Unveiling
the Soul's
Symphony:

A Poetic Journey

BARRINGTON BLACK

Unveiling

The Soul's

Symphony:

A Poetic Journey

BARRINGTON BLACK

508 West 26th Street KEARNEY, NE 68848
402-819-3224
info@medialiteraryexcellence.com

CONTENTS

INTRODUCTION

My name is Barrington, and I am a poet. In the depths of my soul, I find solace and inspiration, weaving words into tapestries of emotions. This autobiography serves as a testament to my poetic journey, specifically focusing on the creation and release of my second book. Roots of Inspiration.

In this chapter, I delve into my early years and explore the seeds of my passion for poetry. From the enchanting stories my grandmother told me to the beauty of nature that surrounded my childhood home, I uncover the roots that nurtured my creative spirit.

My First Book here, I reminisce about the publication of my debut poetry book. The excitement, the doubts, the triumphs, and the lessons learned. I share the evolution of my writing style, the themes that emerged, and the invaluable support I received from readers and fellow poets.

The Second Book takes shape in this chapter, I unveil the birthing process of my second poetry book. From the initial spark of inspiration to the meticulous crafting of each line, I explore the themes, emotions, and experiences that inspired this collection. I touch upon the challenges faced, the revisions made, and the personal growth that occurred during the creative journey.

As the final words of my autobiography flow onto the page, I express my profound gratitude for the opportunity to share my poetic spirit with the world. Through my second book, I hope to touch hearts, spark introspection, and leave an indelible mark on the tapestry of human emotions. With unwavering passion and an ever-evolving voice, I eagerly embrace the path that lies ahead, ready to embark on new poetic adventures.

Reflection in Poem

Whispers of the soul, a gentle plea,
Within the kaleidoscope of emotions set free.
Echoes of eternity, lingering in the air,
Serenade of the heart, a melody rare.

Fragments of dreams, scattered like stars,
In a symphony of words that bridge the scars.
Melodies of the mind, a chorus so sweet,
Guided by shadows and sunbeams we meet.

Reflections in verse, mirrored truth unveiled,
Dancing with the moon, desires never curtailed.
Notes from the universe, whispers in the night,
Painted in poems, colors shining bright.

In a whirlwind of thoughts, chaos and grace,
Whispers in the wind, secrets interlace.
Ink and imagination, boundless and free,
Solitude's symphony, an orchestra just for me.

Songs of the seasons, changing with the tide,
Tangled threads of verse, emotions amplified.
Moments in metaphor, where time stands still,
Soul's soliloquy, an intimate thrill.

Within the pages, a journey unfurls,
Where hearts are touched and souls are heard.
For poetry is the language that sets us free,
To explore the depths of our humanity.

CHAPTER 1
Roots of Inspiration

In this chapter, I delve into my early years and explore the seeds of my passion for poetry. From the enchanting stories my grandmother told me to the beauty of nature that surrounded my childhood home, I uncover the roots that nurtured my creative spirit.

CHAPTER 2
The First Book

Here, I reminisce about the publication of my debut poetry book. The excitement, the doubts, the triumphs, and the lessons learned. I share the evolution of my writing style, the themes that emerged, and the invaluable support I received from readers and fellow poets.

CHAPTER 3
The Second Book Takes Shape

In this chapter, I unveil the birthing process of my second poetry book. From the initial spark of inspiration to the meticulous crafting of each line, I explore the themes, emotions, and experiences that inspired this collection. I touch upon the challenges faced, the revisions made, and the personal growth that occurred during the creative journey.

CHAPTER 4
Reflections and Growth

Here, I reflect upon the evolution of my poetic voice. I delve into the impact of life experiences, my ever-expanding perspectives, and the ways in which my writing has deepened and matured since the publication of my first book. I also share the lessons learned about the art of self-expression and connecting with readers.

CHAPTER 5
Unveiling the Second Book

This chapter centers around the exhilarating moment of releasing my second poetry book to the world. I recount the anticipation, the nerves, and the sense of accomplishment that accompanies the launch. I also touch upon the book's reception, the feedback received, and the emotional connection forged with readers.

CHAPTER 6
The Journey Continues

In the final chapter, I reflect on the impact of my poetry journey on my life and the lives of those who have encountered my words. I share my aspirations for future creative endeavors, the dreams that fuel my pen, and the desire to delve even deeper into the vast realm of poetic expression.

CONCLUSION

As the final words of my autobiography flow onto the page, I express my profound gratitude for the opportunity to share my poetic spirit with the world. Through my second book, I hope to touch hearts, spark introspection, and leave an indelible mark on the tapestry of human emotions. With unwavering passion and an ever-evolving voice, I eagerly embrace the path that lies ahead, ready to embark on new poetic adventures.

Love

In the realm where hearts entwine, behold,
A tapestry woven with love untold.
A symphony of emotions, deep and grand,
A poem that echoes throughout the land.

Love, a gentle breeze, a flame's embrace,
It paints the world with vibrant grace.
An alchemy of souls, a sacred dance,
Where two hearts find their perfect chance.

Love is a language, both spoken and felt,
A melody that makes the heart melt.
It knows no boundaries, no earthly bounds,
And in its presence, all darkness drowns.

It blossoms like flowers in a meadow fair,
With fragrant whispers floating in the air.
It's a beacon of hope, a guiding light,
Leading us through the darkest night.

Love is a symphony of laughter and tears,
A refuge from all our deepest fears.
It lifts us up, empowers our soul,
And makes us feel truly whole.

It's a gentle touch, a tender kiss,
A moment of bliss we simply can't miss.
Love is the answer, the key that unlocks,
The door to a world where hearts beat in sync.

It weaves us together, hand in hand,
Creating a bond that forever will stand.
Through stormy seas and mountains high,
Love perseveres, never asking why.

So let us cherish this gift we've been given,
For in love's embrace, we are truly livin'.
With hearts aflame and spirits aglow,
Love is the greatest story we'll ever know.

Hope

In the depths of despair, where darkness
prevails,
A flicker of light, a beacon, unveils.
It dances with grace, against the night's scope,
A celestial reminder, the essence of hope.

Hope, a whisper that stirs deep within,
A flame that refuses to let dreams rescind.
It surges in hearts, in the face of despair,
Igniting the spirit with courage to bear.

It's a gentle embrace, a soothing balm,
That mends shattered dreams and brings inner
calm.
With each new dawn, hope paints the sky,
Brushing away doubt, letting dreams fly high.

Through trials and tribulations, it holds
steadfast,
A lifeline to cling to when shadows amass.
It fuels resilience, igniting the fire,
To conquer the challenges that life may inspire.

Hope is the compass in the midst of the storm,
Guiding us forward, keeping our hearts warm.
It whispers of possibilities, of dreams yet to be,
Infusing our souls with boundless energy.

With hope as our guide, we'll rise from the fall,
For it nurtures the spirit, mends one and all.

In its gentle embrace, we find the strength,
To conquer adversity, no matter the length.

So let hope be your solace, your guiding light,
A catalyst that propels you to take flight.
Believe in its power, let it fuel your way,
For hope is the promise of a brighter day.

Hate

In the depths of darkness, where shadows reside,
Lurks a poison that spreads, a venomous tide.
Hate, a bitter specter, with a heart filled with scorn,
A destructive force that leaves the spirit torn.

It festers and grows, consumes from within,
Sowing seeds of discord, breeding chaos and sin.
It blinds the eyes to kindness and empathy's call,
Replacing love's embrace with a venomous thrall.

Hate, a raging tempest, fueled by anger's fire,
Leaving compassion and understanding to expire.
It tears at the fabric of unity and peace,
Leaving behind scars that never truly cease.

But let us not surrender, let us rise above,
For hate can be conquered through the power of love.
With open hearts and minds, let us strive,
To heal the wounds inflicted by hate's cruel drive.

For in the face of hatred, we shall stand tall,
Choosing compassion and forgiveness above all.
With empathy as our shield, and love as our guide,
We'll extinguish the flames of hate, far and wide.

15

Let us break the chains that bind us to this
plight,
And embrace the beauty of unity's light.
For hate may linger, but love shall persist,
Until its toxic presence in our world is
dismissed.

So let us join hands, united as one,
And together, let love's victory be won.
For in the battle against hate, we'll find,
That love's enduring power shall always shine.

Mother's

In a mother's embrace, love finds its home,
A bond unbreakable, forever to roam.
A guardian angel, with arms open wide,
A beacon of strength, forever by our side.

A mother's touch, gentle and warm,
Calming our fears, keeping us from harm.
Her soothing words, a lullaby's grace,
Guiding us through life's uncertain chase.

With tender care, she nurtures our dreams,
Instilling in us hope, like sunlight's gleams.
Her unconditional love, a constant embrace,
Filling our hearts with joy and solace.

In her eyes, we see a world of grace,
A reflection of love shining on her face.
Her sacrifices, unnoticed and true,
Unwavering support in all that we do.

A mother's laughter, a melody divine,
A symphony of joy, like sparkling wine.
Her wisdom, a compass in times of despair,
Guiding us through life with utmost care.

In her embrace, we find solace and peace,
A shelter from storms that never cease.
Her love, an eternal flame that burns,
A beacon of hope, wherever one turns.

So let us celebrate mothers, near and far,
The guiding stars that light our way, like a jar.
For in their love, we find strength and grace,
A mother's heart, a treasure we forever embrace.

Father's

In the presence of a father's love, we stand,
A pillar of strength, a steadfast hand.
With wisdom and guidance, he paves the way,
A beacon of light in each passing day.

A father's embrace, both gentle and strong,
An anchor of comfort when things go wrong.
His laughter, a melody that fills the air,
Bringing joy and warmth beyond compare.

With hands that toil and sacrifice,
He builds a foundation, both firm and precise.
He teaches life's lessons, through actions bold,
A role model of virtue, as we unfold.

In his eyes, we glimpse a world of dreams,
A reflection of determination, it seems.
His unwavering support, a constant force,
Guiding us through life's winding course.

A father's presence, a shield from harm,
A shelter of safety, a guiding arm.
His love, a flame that burns ever bright,
Illuminating our path, day and night.

In his words, we find words of wisdom's grace,
Lessons learned, etched upon our hearts'
embrace.
His encouragement, a fuel for our dreams,
Inspiring us to reach beyond our means.

So let us honor fathers, near and far,
The guiding stars that shine, no matter how far.
For in their love, we find strength and pride,
A father's heart, forever by our side.

Daddy's little girl

Daddy's little girl, a bond so pure,
A love that's timeless, steadfast, and sure.
In his arms, she finds solace and peace,
A sanctuary where all worries cease.

Her tiny hand in his, a trust so deep,
Guiding her steps, her secrets to keep.
He's her hero, strong and kind,
A shelter from the storms that unwind.

With a twinkle in his eye and a playful smile,
He lifts her spirits, even for a while.
Their laughter, a symphony, joyful and bright,
Filling their world with pure delight.

He teaches her courage, to stand tall and strong,
To chase her dreams, to right any wrong.
Through his love and support, she finds her way,
Confident and bold, come what may.

Daddy's little girl, a treasure untold,
In his heart, she'll forever hold.
Their bond unbreakable, a lifelong tie,
A love that will never fade or die.

He watches her grow, with pride in his eyes,
Her accomplishments, a source of pure joy.
He's her protector, her rock, her guide,
In his love, she'll forever abide.

So let us celebrate this precious pair,
The bond between a father and daughter so rare.
For in their love, a story unfolds,
Daddy's little girl, a love that forever molds.

Lost

In the depths of shadows, where echoes reside,
I wander alone, with a heavy stride.
A soul adrift, in a world so vast,
Searching for solace from the past.

Lost in the labyrinth of memories untold,
I seek the fragments my heart used to hold.
A tapestry of dreams, now torn and frayed,
Leaving me stranded, feeling betrayed.

Once I danced on the shores of hope,
Where laughter and love would eternally float.
But whispers of time stole moments away,
Leaving me a wanderer, in disarray.

The stars above, once bright and clear,
Now flicker dimly, veiled in fear.
Their gentle glow, once a guiding light,
Now fades into darkness, swallowed by night.

Yet amidst the haze, a flicker remains,
A beacon of hope, through sorrow and pains.
For in the depths of loss, I find my voice,
A strength to endure, a reason to rejoice.

Though the road is treacherous, and I may
stumble,
I'll gather the fragments and never crumble.
For in each tear shed, a resilience is born,
A strength that emerges, weathered and worn.

In the tapestry of life, losses are woven,
But strength arises when we remain unbroken.
And though I may wander, lost in the fray,
I'll embrace the unknown, and find my own way.

For in the heart's depths, where darkness
resides,
A flicker of light, forever abides.
And through the journey, no matter the cost,
I'll rise from the ashes, never truly lost.

Baby

*I*n the cradle of innocence, a miracle unfolds,
A precious little being, with a love yet untold.
A baby's laughter, like a symphony so sweet,
Filling hearts with joy, making life complete.

Tiny fingers, reaching out to touch,
A world of wonder they yearn to clutch.
Eyes so bright, with curiosity ablaze,
Exploring new horizons, in their own little ways.

A baby's smile, a glimpse of pure delight,
Melting hearts with its radiance, shining so
bright.
Their laughter, like music, fills the air,
A melody of innocence, beyond compare.

In the embrace of a mother's loving arms,
A baby finds solace, safe from all harms.
Nurtured and cherished, they grow with each
day,
Blossoming like a flower, in a beautiful display.

Their first steps, a triumph, a moment to
treasure,
Cheered on by loved ones, hearts bursting with
pleasure.
Their babbling words, a language all their own,
A symphony of babble, a love that's grown.

Oh, the wonders a baby brings,

A world of possibilities, on fragile wings.
They teach us patience, and the purest kind of
love,
Guiding us to see the beauty in the world above.

So let us celebrate the miracle of new life,
With tender care and love, amidst the strife.
For in a baby's presence, we find hope anew,
A promise of a future, bright and true.

Time

Time, a silent river that ceaselessly flows,
An intangible force, as it ebbs and it slows.
A constant companion, yet elusive and fleet,
It shapes our existence with its rhythmic beat.

A tapestry woven with moments untold,
Time weaves the stories of young and old.
It dances through seasons, in a waltz of its own,
Marking the milestones as they're etched in
stone.

It whispers in the wind, as days turn to years,
Leaving imprints of laughter, of joy, and of tears.
With each passing second, it slips through our
hands,
Reminding us gently of life's shifting sands.

In the cradle of morning, it paints a new dawn,
A canvas of possibilities, waiting to be drawn.
It urges us forward, to seize every day,
For time waits for no one, as it silently slips
away.

Yet time is not bound by the ticking of clocks,
It's the memories we cherish, the key to life's
locks.
It's the laughter we share, the moments we hold
dear,
In the tapestry of time, it's the love that we
revere.

And in the twilight hours, as day turns to night,
Time weaves a symphony of stars shining bright.
It whispers of dreams, of the stories yet untold,
As we navigate its currents, both the young and
the old.

So let us embrace time, with gratitude and grace,
For it's in the present that life finds its place.
Let us savor each moment, as it unfolds,
For time is a treasure, more precious than gold.

For in the tapestry of life, time weaves its thread,
Leading us forward, where paths may have led.
So let us honor its passage, with hearts held
high,
For time is a gift, meant to be lived, not to pass
by.

Marriage

Two souls entwined, a journey begun,
In the sacred bond of love, two lives become one.
Marriage, a tapestry woven with care,
A union of hearts, a promise to share.

Through laughter and tears, hand in hand,
Together they walk, on life's shifting sand.
In the dance of togetherness, they find their
grace,
Navigating the challenges, with love as their
base.

Like a garden nurtured with tender embrace,
Marriage blossoms, adorned with beauty and
grace.
Through seasons of change, they weather the
storm,
For love is the shelter, safe and warm.

In the depths of understanding, they find solace,
A refuge in each other, a harbor in the chaos.
They celebrate victories, both big and small,
For in marriage's embrace, they stand tall.

The vows they exchanged, a sacred decree,
To love and to cherish, forever to be.
Through joys and sorrows, they steadfastly
stand,
Bound by a love that's built to withstand.

In the ebb and flow of life's ceaseless tide,
They grow together, side by side.
Companions, lovers, and best friends too,
In marriage's embrace, dreams come true.

They learn to compromise, to forgive and mend,
For in unity and compassion, hearts can
transcend.
For marriage is a tapestry, woven with trust,
A commitment to love, an unbreakable thrust.

So let us honor the beauty of this sacred bond,
A testament to love, forever beyond.
May marriages thrive, with love as their guide,
And may they journey together, with hearts
unified.

Honesty

In a world of masks and hidden guise,
Honesty emerges as a beacon that never dies.
A virtue so pure, it shines with inner light,
Guiding us through darkness, with its truth so
bright.

Honesty, a mirror that reflects the soul,
Revealing our essence, making us whole.
It speaks with clarity, unburdened and clear,
Dispelling illusions, erasing all fear.

With honesty as our compass, we navigate life's
sea,
Guided by integrity, unafraid to be free.
It builds bridges of trust, connecting hearts as
one,
For honesty is the foundation on which
relationships are spun.

It's the courage to admit when we're wrong,
To face our flaws, and grow strong.
To speak our truth, even when it's hard,
For honesty is the catalyst that mends the
scarred.

In a world of pretense, where facades prevail,
Honesty stands tall, refusing to derail.
It strips away veils, revealing what's true,
For honesty cuts through the fog, with a piercing
view.

Yet honesty is gentle, a compassionate force,
It seeks understanding, and stays on its course.
It fosters empathy, and nurtures respect,
For honesty is a virtue that we should protect.

So let us embrace the power of honesty's might,
And stand in its presence, bathed in its light.
For with honesty as our guide, we find our way,
To a world of authenticity, where truth holds
sway.

In the realm of honesty, we find liberation,
A path of integrity, a soul's elevation.
For honesty, dear friend, is a treasure untold,
A gift we must cherish, a virtue to behold.

Christmas

In the hush of winter's embrace, a joyous
season nears,
When hearts are warmed by love, and hope
replaces fears.
The air is filled with whispers, of a magical
delight,
As Christmas paints the world, in colors pure
and bright.

A symphony of carols, floating through the
night,
Filling every corner, with melodies of delight.
Voices raised in harmony, spreading peace and
cheer,
For Christmas brings together, the ones we hold
dear.

In the twinkle of lights, adorning every tree,
A shimmering reminder, of the love that sets us
free.
Each ornament a story, a cherished memory,
Binding us together, in a tapestry of unity.

Through the frost-kissed windows, snowflakes
gently dance,
Creating a wonderland, a whimsical romance.
Children's laughter fills the air, with innocent
delight,
As they dream of Santa's sleigh, on this
enchanted night.

The aroma of cinnamon, of cookies freshly
baked,
Fills homes with warmth, and love that's never
faked.
Families gather 'round, by the fire's tender glow,
Sharing tales and laughter, hearts all aglow.

But Christmas is more than just presents and
décor,
It's a time for compassion, a reminder to restore,
The bonds that connect us, in a world so vast,
To spread kindness and love, and make
moments last.

For in the heart of Christmas, lies a timeless
truth,
That love can heal and mend, in a world
uncouth.
It's a season of giving, of selflessness and grace,
A reminder of the joy, in embracing every face.

So let us celebrate Christmas, with hearts open
wide,
Embracing the spirit, that in us will abide.
May love be our guiding star, shining from
above,
And fill our lives with blessings, and everlasting
love.

Work

In the realm where toil and labor reside,
Where dreams are forged and passions collide,
A tapestry woven with threads of sweat,
I shall pen a poem, a tribute to the work we get.

Beneath the morning sun's gentle embrace,
We rise with purpose and a steadfast pace.
The world awakens, bustling and alive,
And into the workforce, we eagerly dive.

With sleeves rolled up and determination ablaze,
We embark upon the path of our working days.
From towering buildings to fields so vast,
Our efforts merge, present and future cast.

In offices, minds dance with thoughts so bright,
As keyboards tap and screens illuminate the
night.
Ideas take flight, a symphony of innovation,
A collective endeavor to shape our civilization.

In factories, the rhythmic hum of machines,
Crafting marvels with precision, it seems.
Hands and gears in harmonious accord,
Creating wonders that strike a resonant chord.

On the roads, wheels turning without a pause,
Delivering goods, connecting distant shores.
Traversing miles, bridging gaps with speed,
A testament to the strength of human need.

From the hospitals where healing hands reside,
To classrooms where knowledge is our guide,
In every profession, a purpose we find,
A chance to make a difference, to leave a mark
behind.

But amidst the toil, let us not forget,
The importance of balance, lest we regret.
To work with passion and take time to rest,
To nourish our souls and be at our best.

For work is not merely a means to an end,
But a journey of growth, a message to send.
With each task accomplished, we learn and grow,
And in the process, our true selves we come to
know.

So let us celebrate the work we do,
With gratitude, purpose, and spirits anew.
For in the realm where toil and labor reside,
We find fulfillment, and our souls take pride.

Natures

In the realm where nature's wonders unfold,
Where beauty reigns, captivating and bold,
I shall compose a poem, a tribute to its grace,
A melody of words in this sacred space.

Beneath the cerulean sky's expansive dome,
Where birds soar freely, finding their home,
Mountains rise with grandeur, reaching the skies,
And valleys embrace, where serenity lies.

In forests deep, where sunlight filters through,
A tapestry of green, a sanctuary anew,
Whispering leaves share secrets untold,
As ancient trees stand tall, wise and bold.

The rivers flow, their melodies so sweet,
Carving paths through land, a rhythmic beat,
They nourish the earth, with life they imbue,
A symphony of water, ever pure and true.

The ocean vast, a world of mystery untamed,
With waves that crash and gentle breezes named,
Within its depths, a kaleidoscope of life,
An ecosystem thriving, amidst depths so rife.

Flowers bloom, a vibrant burst of hues,
Their fragrances captivating, chasing away the
blues,
They paint the meadows, a canvas so divine,
A testament to nature's art, an ode to time.

Creatures roam, from the mighty to the small,
In harmony they coexist, answering nature's call,
From the graceful deer to the soaring eagle,
Each holds a place, in this sacred regal.

Oh, nature! You captivate with your grand
design,
A masterpiece of wonder, ever so fine,
May we cherish and protect, with hearts aligned,
For in your embrace, true solace we find.

Let us tread lightly upon your hallowed ground,
Listen to your wisdom, in whispers profound,
For in your embrace, we find solace and peace,
A reminder of our place, a love that won't cease.

In the realm where nature's wonders unfold,
Where beauty reigns, captivating and bold,
I offer this poem, a humble homage to thee,
Nature's eternal song, an ode to the free.

Sadnesses

In the realm where sadness casts its shadow,

Where tears flow freely, and hearts lie low,
I shall weave a poem, to embrace the pain,
To honor the emotions that often wane.

Oh, sadness, you cloak us in your embrace,
A heavy burden upon our souls, a somber space,
You descend upon us with a weight so deep,
A tempest of emotions, difficult to keep.

In moments of sorrow, we find ourselves lost,
In a labyrinth of feelings, the tempest's cost,
Like raindrops falling from a darkened sky,
You seep into our hearts, leaving us wondering
why.

Sometimes you arrive as a gentle drizzle,
A melancholic melody that makes us fizzle,
Other times, you storm with thunderous might,
Engulfing us in darkness, blurring day and night.

Yet within your depths, a purpose lies,
A catalyst for growth, a chance to rise,
You teach us empathy, to embrace each other's
pain,
To hold hands in solidarity, and mend what's
been strained.

For in the tapestry of life, you have your place,
A contrast to joy, a reminder to embrace,

To appreciate the moments of happiness so
dear,
And to lend a compassionate ear.

Oh, sadness, though you weigh upon our chest,
You remind us of our humanity, our very best,
Through tears and struggles, we learn to heal,
To find strength within, and to truly feel.

So let us not shun you or push you away,
But welcome your presence, as night welcomes
day,
For in acknowledging you, we find release,
And pave the way for a heart at peace.

In the realm where sadness casts its shadow,
Where tears flow freely, and hearts lie low,
This poem stands, a tribute to your might,
A reminder that even in darkness, there is still
light.

Fear

In the realm where fear holds its dominion,

Where shadows dance and hearts feel the pinion,
I shall pen a poem, an exploration profound,
To understand fear's grip, its whispers resound.

Oh, fear, you're a specter that looms so near,
A primal instinct, caution crystal clear,
You manifest in myriad forms and guise,
With trembling steps, we face you, wise.

In the face of the unknown, you arise,
Casting doubt and worry, obscuring skies,
You whisper doubts in the corners of the mind,
A relentless adversary, often unkind.

You freeze our steps, impede our flight,
A weight upon the chest, an eternal fight,
But within your clutches, strength takes birth,
A catalyst for courage, a chance for worth.

Fear, you're a teacher, albeit severe,
Guiding us to confront what we hold dear,
You push us beyond the boundaries we've set,
To discover resilience, to never forget.

Yet, sometimes you become a prison cell,
Restricting dreams, a foreboding spell,
But in the depths of darkness, hope ignites,
A flickering flame, dispelling your nights.

For in the realm where fear's tendrils creep,
Hope and bravery rise from slumber deep,
With each step forward, fear loses its might,
As we embrace uncertainty, bathed in light.

So let us acknowledge your presence, fear,
But not let you dictate what we hold dear,
For in the face of fear, we find our might,
To transform darkness into radiant light.

$\mathcal{B}$itterness

$\mathcal{I}$n the realm where bitterness takes its place,

Where resentment lingers, leaving a bitter taste,
I shall compose a poem, to explore its hold,
To unravel its layers, its story to unfold.

Oh, bitterness, you are a poison, deep and
strong,
A lingering ache that seeps into every song,
You take root in hearts, like thorny vines,
Entangling emotions, poisoning the lines.

With every bitter word, you sow discontent,
Creating rifts, where harmony was once sent,
You feed on grievances, nurturing the pain,
Blurring the path to forgiveness, in disdain.

Bitterness, you're a weight that burdens the soul,
A constant reminder of wounds that take their
toll,
You color perceptions, tainting the view,
And hinder healing, blocking the path anew.

But in the depths of bitterness, a lesson lies,
A chance for growth, a bridge to empathize,
For when we taste the bitterness of our own
strife,
We learn compassion, the essence of a
meaningful life.

Let us not be consumed by bitterness' snare,

But seek understanding, and the burden share,
For in forgiveness and letting go, we find release,
And pave the way for inner peace.

Oh, bitterness, though you grip with might,
We choose to rise above, to seek the light,
To replace bitterness with kindness and grace,
Embracing love's warmth, leaving no trace.

In the realm where bitterness claims its space,
Where resentment lingers, leaving a bitter taste,
This poem stands, a reminder to let go,
To cultivate compassion and let bitterness flow.

Loyalty

Like sturdy roots that anchor a tree,
Loyalty binds souls, forever free.
Through trials and tribulations, it prevails,
A shield against doubt, a ship that sails.

In friendship's garden, a blossoming bloom,
Loyalty, a fragrance that banishes gloom.
A bond unbreakable, through thick and thin,
A sanctuary of trust that dwells within.

In love's embrace, a flame that burns bright,
Loyalty's flame, a guiding light.
Through tempests and storms, it stands tall,
A sheltering refuge, for one and all.

In days of darkness, when shadows creep,
Loyalty's vigil, it does keep.
A guardian angel, with unwavering might,
Guiding lost souls back to the light.

In loyalty, oaths are eternally sworn,
A sacred promise, never to be torn.
With honor and valor, it takes its stand,
A testament to courage, hand in hand.

Oh, loyalty, you are a treasure untold,
A melody of loyalty, forever unfold.
In this symphony of hearts, let us rejoice,
Embracing loyalty, with one united voice.

So let us cherish, this virtue so rare,
For loyalty's flame, forever we'll bear.
Through time and space, our spirits will soar,
Bound by loyalty, forevermore.

I need a girl

In the realm of dreams, where wishes are spun,
I seek a girl, a radiant sun.
With grace and charm, like a gentle breeze,
A soul that brings me to my knees.

I need a girl, a companion true,
To share life's joys, both old and new.
With eyes that sparkle, bright and clear,
A heart that's kind, forever near.

I need a girl, with laughter so sweet,
Whose smile can make my world complete.
In her presence, my worries fade away,
Her laughter, like music, brightens each day.

I need a girl, with a spirit so free,
Who dances through life with wild glee.
With passion ablaze, she follows her dreams,
Illuminating the path with vibrant beams.

I need a girl, whose touch brings peace,
Whose gentle caress brings sweet release.
A hand to hold, when darkness invades,
Together we'll conquer, unyielding as blades.

I need a girl, with a voice so pure,
Whose words inspire, so gentle and sure.
With wisdom beyond her tender years,
She's a beacon of light, dispelling all fears.

I need a girl, whose love is profound,
A love that knows no bounds.
With her, I'll build a world so grand,
Hand in hand, we'll forever stand.

In this vast universe, I yearn to find,
The girl who'll share this heart of mine.
So I'll wait with hope, and trust in fate,
For the girl I need, who'll make life great.

Pain and love

*I*n the realm of emotions, where hearts collide,
There exists a dance, where love and pain reside.
A complex tango, intertwined and entwined,
A bittersweet symphony, where souls are
aligned.

Love, a flame that ignites the darkest night,
A celestial fire, burning ever so bright.
It paints the world with vibrant hues,
Filling our hearts with joy we can't refuse.

But intertwined with love, pain finds its way,
A shadowy companion, night and day.
For love's tender touch can bring both delight,
And moments of anguish, like stars in the night.

Love's tender whispers can heal and mend,
Yet it also has the power to break and rend.
For when hearts shatter, pain takes its toll,
Leaving scars that linger, a wounded soul.

But pain, too, holds a purpose profound,
It teaches us lessons, it shapes us, I've found.
Through heartache and trials, we learn and grow,
Emerging stronger, with a resilience that shows.

Love and pain, a delicate dance they weave,
In the tapestry of life, they both believe.
For love wouldn't be as sweet without its sting,
And pain wouldn't hurt if love didn't bring.

So let us embrace both love and pain,
For they are intertwined, like sunshine and rain.
In the depths of sorrow, love's light can guide,
And through pain's embrace, love's strength will abide.

For in the tapestry of life's grand design,
Love and pain entwine, forever entwined.
And through the highs and lows, we'll rise above,
Embracing the beauty of both, in the name of love.

How could you leave us

In the realm of sorrow, where tears freely flow,
I ask the question, "How could you go?"
A void now lingers, where your presence once
thrived,
Leaving us broken, feeling so deprived.

How could you leave us, without a goodbye?
Leaving our hearts heavy, questioning why.
The pain sears within, a relentless ache,
Our world turned upside down, a soul-shattering
quake.

We search for answers in the depths of our grief,
Seeking solace, seeking some relief.
But the echoes of your absence ring loud and
clear,
Leaving us grasping for memories held dear.

You were a light, a beacon in our lives,
With love and laughter that forever survives.
Your smile, a warmth that could melt any strife,
Now a cherished memory, etched in our life.

The emptiness now fills every space,
A void that time cannot erase.
We yearn for your presence, your comforting
embrace,
But all that remains are your footsteps and trace.

Though you may have departed, your spirit lives
on,
In the hearts that loved you, the bonds that
won't be gone.
We'll carry your light, in our memories we'll
keep,
Embracing the love, in our hearts so deep.

So though the pain persists, and tears may fall,
We'll find the strength to stand tall.
For you have left an indelible mark,
Forever engraved, even in the dark.

How could you leave us? The question remains,
But love transcends, and still remains.
In our hearts, you'll forever reside,
A guiding star, our eternal guide.

Sacrifice

Selflessness, where heroes are born,
Resides a noble act, a sacrifice adorn.
A choice made willingly, for the greater good,
A testament of courage, as true heroes should.

Sacrifice, a beacon of light in the night,
An offering made, to make a wrong right.
It whispers of love, in its purest form,
A selfless surrender, against any norm.

A parent's sacrifice, nurturing and strong,
Pouring their heart into a child's lifelong song.
Forgoing their dreams, putting others first,
Their love an eternal flame, never to be reversed.

A soldier's sacrifice, on a battlefield's crest,
Marching with valor, their duty they invest.
Leaving behind home, family, and peace,
To protect and defend, their sacrifice won't
cease.

A friend's sacrifice, a shoulder to lean,
Listening, supporting, wiping tears unseen.
Giving their time, their presence, their care,
A bond unbreakable, a love beyond compare.

Sacrifice, a choice made with open eyes,
To lift others up, to silence their cries.
It humbles the soul, and ignites a fire,
To make a difference, to lift spirits higher.

But let us not forget, in sacrifice's embrace,
The strength it requires, the tears it may trace.
For it comes at a cost, a personal toll,
Yet heroes emerge, with a steadfast soul.

So let us honor those who sacrifice,
Their love, their courage, their unyielding ties.
For in their selflessness, we find our way,
To a world where compassion will always hold
sway.

In the realm of selflessness, let our hearts be led,
By the echoes of sacrifice, where true heroes
tread.
For it is through sacrifice, we learn to give,
And in giving, we find the true meaning to live.

Forgiveness

Healing, where wounds run deep,
Resides a powerful act, forgiveness we keep.
A balm for the heart, a soothing embrace,
A choice to let go, and find inner peace.

Forgiveness, a beacon in the darkest night,
A bridge to mend what was once broken and
tight.
It doesn't erase the pain or the past,
But it sets us free, releasing burdens amassed.

To forgive is to release the chains that bind,
To find liberation, a tranquil state of mind.
It's a gift we give ourselves, a chance to heal,
To move forward, allowing wounds to seal.

Forgiveness doesn't mean forgetting the pain,
But rather, it opens the door to growth again.
It's a step towards empathy, compassion's
embrace,
A willingness to understand, a gesture of grace.

In forgiveness, we find strength and resilience,
A path to freedom, breaking the cycle of
vengeance.
It's a choice to rise above, to let love prevail,
To dissolve bitterness, and let kindness set sail.

Forgiveness is a journey, it takes time and care,
It requires courage, vulnerability to bear.

But the rewards are immense, a weight lifted
away,
As forgiveness brings light to a brand-new day.

So let us embrace forgiveness, with open hearts,
Releasing the shackles, allowing healing to start.
For in forgiveness, we find peace's sweet song,
And in forgiving others, we, too, become strong.

In the realm of healing, forgiveness abides,
A powerful force that restores and guides.
May we learn to forgive, and be forgiven too,
Creating a world where compassion shines
through.

My stress

Stress, my mind does dwell,
A tempest of emotions, a chaotic spell.
Like thunderous clouds that darken my sky,
It weighs upon my shoulders, makes me sigh.

The world spins fast, a relentless race,
Demands and expectations I must embrace.
But within my heart, a weariness grows,
As anxiety takes hold, my spirit it slows.

The weight upon my chest, heavy and cruel,
A constant battle, an internal duel.
Sleepless nights, restless thoughts invade,
My mind a battleground, where worries cascade.

But amidst the storm, a glimmer of light,
A beacon of hope, shining so bright.
For in the darkness, I find my release,
Through words and rhythm, my soul finds
peace.

I pour my stress onto the page,
In lines of ink, my thoughts engage.
A poem unfolds, a soothing balm,
As I navigate the labyrinth of calm.

Each word a brushstroke, painting my pain,
Transforming stress into a gentle rain.
The rhythm guides me, a steady beat,
Leading me to a place of retreat.

Through metaphors and verses, I find reprieve,
As my stress unravels, I start to believe.
That within my heart, there's strength untold,
To face the challenges, to be bold.

So, I write and write, until my stress is gone,
Transformed into verses, a melodic song.
For poetry is my refuge, my sanctuary,
A healing art that sets my spirit free.

In the realm of stress, I'll always find solace,
With pen in hand, I'll embrace the challenge.
For through my words, I'll conquer the unrest,
And find serenity within my poetic quest.

Friendship

Friendship, a treasure so rare and true,

A bond so strong, between me and you.
Through the seasons, through highs and lows,
Our friendship blossoms, and it only grows.

In the garden of life, we found each other,
Like flowers entwined, we support one another.
Through laughter and tears, joy and strife,
We navigate this journey, hand in hand, side by
side.

Through thick and thin, we stand tall,
Building memories, like a grand brick wall.
We share our dreams, our hopes, our fears,
In the tapestry of friendship, we weave the years.

A friend is a pillar, when the world feels unkind,
A sheltering tree, where solace we find.
In your presence, I feel truly seen,
Accepted and cherished, for who I have been.

We celebrate victories, big and small,
And catch each other if ever we fall.
A listening ear, a comforting embrace,
In the warmth of friendship, we find our grace.

Through conversations, both deep and light,
We paint our stories, in colors so bright.
We laugh, we dance, we sing and play,
Friendship's melodies brighten each day.

Distance may separate us, oceans wide,
Yet, our bond remains strong, cannot be denied.
With every message, call, or heartfelt letter,
Our friendship continues to grow and get better.

So, here's to friendship, a gift so divine,
A treasure that only few are lucky to find.
May it endure, forever and evermore,
A beacon of love, forever to adore.

In this beautiful symphony, we are friends,
Bound by a love, that never ends.
In the tapestry of life, our threads entwine,
Forever and always, dear friend of mine.

Courage

In the face of darkness, where shadows creep,
Courage emerges, from within we leap.
A flame ignites, a fire deep inside,
Guiding us forward, our fears defied.

Courage is not the absence of fear,
But the strength to persevere,
To stand tall, when the world seems bleak,
And find the power we thought we'd seek.

It's taking that step into the unknown,
With trembling legs, but a heart full-blown.
To face the challenges that lie ahead,
With determination, we forge ahead.

In the depths of doubt, courage is found,
A flickering light, a reassuring sound.
It whispers, "You have what it takes,
To conquer mountains, to cross the lakes."

It's the voice that says, "You can try again,
Embrace the struggle, learn to ascend.
For every failure is a chance to grow,
To face your fears, let your true self show."

Courage is found in the quiet moments,
When we choose to rise, despite our opponents.
To speak our truth, to defend what's right,
Even when the world is consumed by night.

It's the strength to stand up for the weak,
To fight for justice, to hear their plea.
To lend a hand, be a guiding light,
And make a difference, no matter how slight.

Courage is the warrior within our soul,
Unyielding, relentless, making us whole.
It fuels our dreams, ignites our desire,
To reach for the stars, to aim higher.

So, let courage be your faithful guide,
In every battle, by your side.
Embrace its power, let it lead the way,
And you'll conquer the challenges that come
your way.

For within you lies a fearless heart,
Ready to unleash its courageous art.
Embrace the call, let your spirit soar,
And courage will carry you forevermore.

Any love

In a world of love, where hearts entwine,
I've searched for a love that is truly mine.
But amidst the chaos, I've come to see,
That any love that ain't you, can never be.

For in your presence, I find a home,
A love that's genuine, no need to roam.
Your touch, your smile, they set me free,
In your embrace, I discover the real me.

In the tapestry of hearts, I've known a few,
But none compare to the love I've found in you.
They were fleeting flames, flickering and dim,
But with you, love burns bright from within.

Any love that ain't you, is a mere illusion,
A counterfeit sparkle, a shallow infusion.
For your love is authentic, deep and pure,
A connection so strong, forever endure.

In your eyes, I see a reflection of truth,
A love that's unwavering, a timeless proof.
With every beat of my heart, I long for your
touch,
For in your love, I've found my soul's crutch.

No other love can fill this void,
For any love that ain't you, is quickly destroyed.
You are my compass, my guiding light,
With you, love feels effortless, oh so right.

So, let the world offer its temporary charms,
I'll remain steadfast, safe within your arms.
For any love that ain't you, holds no sway,
I choose your love, each and every day.

In your love, I've discovered my truth,
A love that's everlasting, unbreakable, and
smooth.
For any love that ain't you, can never be,
Because, my love, you are the one true key.

Angry

In the depths of anger, a tempest roars,
A storm within, crashing on distant shores.
Emotions surge, like a fiery tide,
Engulfing reason, where peace once resided.

The flames of fury dance and consume,
Transforming tranquility into a fiery fume.
The heart pounds, fists clench tight,
As anger takes hold, blinding the sight.

The world turns red, as rage takes its place,
A torrential downpour, an unyielding chase.
Words fly like arrows, sharp and cruel,
Fueling the fire, a destructive duel.

But in the midst of anger's fierce reign,
A glimmer of awareness, a flicker of pain.
For anger, though forceful, will not sustain,
It leaves behind scars, a lingering stain.

In the aftermath, regret may seep,
As the flames of anger start to sleep.
Reflection sets in, a moment of pause,
To mend the wounds, to find a cause.

For anger is a messenger, a signal to heed,
A call to examine, to fulfill a need.
To seek understanding, to find a way,
To transform anger into a gentler display.

In the realm of anger, let wisdom befriend,
A pathway to healing, a chance to transcend.
To channel the energy, to rise above,
And replace anger's grip with compassion and
love.

So, let anger be a catalyst for change,
To break free from its destructive range.
Embrace self-awareness, choose a peaceful
stride,
And let empathy and understanding be your
guide.

For anger, though potent, can be transformed,
Into a force for good, where bridges are formed.
Let it be a catalyst for growth and insight,
And find serenity beyond anger's might.

Soul

In the realm where dreams unfold,
Where emotions dance and stories are told,
There reside souls, ethereal and deep,
Whispering secrets that they keep.

Each soul a tapestry, woven with grace,
A symphony of colors, in time and space,
With every breath, a story they bear,
Of joy, of sorrow, and love's tender care.

Some souls are wild, like a raging flame,
Burning with passion, never the same,
They soar through skies, untouched by fear,
Leaving trails of brilliance, crystal-clear.

Others are gentle, like a babbling brook,
Flowing through valleys, with a tranquil look,
They nurture hearts with kindness untold,
Their compassion, a balm for the soul.

There are souls that weep, with wounds unseen,
Carrying burdens, their spirits keen,
Yet through the pain, they find their way,
Turning darkness into dawn's golden ray.

Some souls are seekers, forever in quest,
Exploring horizons, they never rest,
They chase the stars, and the mysteries they
hold,
Their boundless curiosity, a tale yet untold.

And there are souls, ancient and wise,
With depth in their gaze, like ancient skies,
They carry the wisdom of ages past,
Guiding lost souls, helping them amass.

Souls intertwine, like a cosmic dance,
Connected by threads, a timeless expanse,
In this tapestry of life, we find our place,
A symphony of souls, bound by grace.

So honor the souls you meet on your way,
For each has a story, a role to play,
Embrace their essence, let your soul be known,
For in this intricate web, we are not alone.

The strength to hold on to your heart

When storms of doubt come crashing in,
And shadows of fear begin to spin,
Wrap yourself in courage's embrace,
And hold on to your heart's sacred space.

For hearts are fragile, tender and true,
Vulnerable to pain, yet resilient too,
They beat with hope, with dreams and desire,
A flame that burns, an eternal fire.

When betrayal leaves scars upon your soul,
And trust becomes a distant goal,
Gather the fragments, piece by piece,
And hold on to your heart's inner peace.

Let not the bitterness of past wounds,
Define the present, where love blooms,
Embrace forgiveness, let go of strife,
And hold on to your heart's boundless life.

In moments of darkness, when shadows loom,
And life's burdens cast a heavy gloom,
Summon the strength, deep from within,
And hold on to your heart, where love begins.

For love is a tapestry, woven with care,
A treasure to cherish, a bond to bear,
Nurture it gently, through joy and through pain,
And hold on to your heart, the love will remain.

So, dear soul, when life's tempests start,
When doubts assail and tear you apart,
Remember the power that lies in your chest,
And hold on to your heart, it knows what's best.

For in the depths of your being, you'll find,
The resilience, the love, the strength combined,
Hold on to your heart, let it guide your way,
And love's enduring flame will never sway.

Joyful

In the realm of boundless delight,
Where laughter dances, shining bright,
There blooms a garden, vibrant and free,
A symphony of joy for all to see.

With every sunrise, a new day begins,
Bathing the world in colors that grin,
The birds sing melodies, pure and clear,
Filling the air with blissful cheer.

In fields of flowers, petals unfold,
Painting the landscape in hues of gold,
Their fragrant whispers, a sweet embrace,
Inviting us to dance in nature's grace.

Children's laughter, like bells in the air,
Infectious and pure, without a care,
Their playful spirits, a radiant beam,
Igniting the joy that makes hearts gleam.

In gentle breezes, joy takes flight,
Caressing our souls, like wings of light,
It kisses our cheeks, with a tender touch,
Filling our hearts with love's vibrant rush.

Joy resides in moments, big and small,
In friendships that deepen, binding us all,
In acts of kindness, freely given,
In the simple joys that make life worth living.

It dances in music, a rhythmic delight,
Melodies that lift us to soaring heights,
In dance and movement, a joyful release,
Allowing our spirits to find perfect peace.

So let us embrace this gift we've found,
Let joy's symphony resound,
In every laugh, in every smile,
Let joy be our compass, our guiding mile.

For joy is the song that sets us free,
A precious gift for you and me,
So let our hearts, forever sing,
In the symphony of joy, let happiness ring.

Cheated

In the shadows of deceit and lies,
Where trust is shattered and love defies,
There lies a wounded heart, torn apart,
Betrayed and broken, a cheated heart.

Once a flame burned with passion bright,
Two souls entwined, love's pure delight,
But secrets whispered, a deceitful game,
Left a heart wounded, consumed by shame.

Promises made with empty words,
A web of deception skillfully blurred,
The pain inflicted cuts deep and true,
Leaving scars unseen, a haunting hue.

Yet from the darkness, strength shall rise,
A phoenix soaring through stormy skies,
A cheated heart, though bruised and sore,
Shall mend its pieces, to love once more.

Through tears of anguish, lessons are learned,
Boundaries set, bridges rebuilt, bridges burned,
Forgiveness sought, a path to healing,
A chance to grow, a chance at revealing.

For cheating's touch may leave a stain,
But it cannot define, nor cause disdain,
A cheated heart can rise above,
Embracing self-worth, reclaiming love.

So let the pain be a teacher's call,
A catalyst for growth, standing tall,
For in the depths of a cheated soul,
Resides the strength to once again be whole.

And as the wounds heal, scars will fade,
A new dawn emerges, a serenade,
A cheated heart, now wise and strong,
Prevails over darkness, finding where it belongs.

So hold your head high, let the past unwind,
For a cheated heart, in time, shall find,
That love's true essence, pure and deep,
Can mend the wounds and restore its leap.

Journey

On the canvas of life, a journey unfolds,
A tapestry woven with stories untold,
Through valleys and mountains, both near and
far,
We embark on a quest beneath sun and stars.

With each step we take, a new world is found,
In the footsteps of giants, on hallowed ground,
We wander through moments, fleeting yet grand,
Exploring the vastness of this wondrous land.

The road may be winding, filled with unknown,
Yet courage within us continues to grow,
For in every challenge, strength finds its birth,
And the fire within us ignites our worth.

We meet fellow travelers along the way,
Sharing laughter and tears, night and day,
Their stories intertwine with ours, for a while,
Creating connections that make our hearts smile.

The journey reveals both triumph and strife,
Lessons we learn, shaping our life,
We stumble, we fall, but we rise again,
Transformed by the journey, resilient and ten.

Through deserts of doubt, we seek our truth,
Through forests of fear, we find our youth,
The path may be treacherous, steep and steep,
But the beauty lies in the secrets we keep.

Oh, the places we go, the sights we behold,
From shimmering oceans to cities of gold,
From quiet retreats to bustling streets,
Our journey unfolds, a symphony sweet.

And as we continue, day by day,
The journey reveals its purpose and sway,
For it's not just the destination we seek,
But the growth, the wisdom, the soul's mystique.

So embrace the journey, with open arms,
Embrace the unknown, its unpredictable charms,
For in every step, a story is born,
And the journey itself becomes our adorn.

So let us wander, let us explore,
The depths of our being, forevermore,
For it is in the journey, we truly find,
The magic of life, the journey of a kind.

Lifeless

In the realm of shadows, where darkness
resides,
Lies a sense of emptiness, where life subsides,
A barren landscape, devoid of light,
A symphony of silence, a lifeless plight.

In the absence of color, the world turns gray,
A desolate canvas where hope fades away,
The echoes of laughter, now distant and cold,
Aching hearts yearn for stories untold.

Lifeless whispers fill the air,
Like hollow echoes of a forgotten prayer,
Dreams once vibrant, now lie in decay,
Lost in the void, fading away.

The soul, once aflame, now feels so numb,
Like a withered flower, unable to bloom,
Passion extinguished, a flickering flame,
A lifeless existence, devoid of aim.

But in the depths of life's darkest hour,
A glimmer of light can still have power,
A single spark, a gentle caress,
Can breathe life into the lifeless, to bless.

For even in shadows, hope can arise,
A phoenix awakening, ready to rise,
From ashes of despair, a rebirth unfolds,
A resurrection of life, as the story unfolds.

So let us seek the light, in the depths of despair,
Embrace the journey, with courage to bear,
For even in darkness, life can be found,
Like a symphony of whispers, a soft, gentle
sound.

Let us breathe life into the lifeless soul,
With love and compassion, our hearts made
whole,
For in the dance of existence, we find our worth,
A reminder that life, even in darkness, can birth.

So let us cherish the moments, both big and
small,
Embrace the beauty, the wonders that call,
For life, though fragile, is a precious gift,
A chance to ignite the lifeless, to uplift.

For within our souls, a fire does burn,
Yearning for life's lessons, eager to learn,
And in the embrace of love, we shall find,
That even in lifelessness, hope is enshrined.

Uplifting

In a world of shadows, where hope seems lost,
A spark ignites, no matter the cost.
For in our hearts, a fire burns bright,
Guiding us onward through darkest night.

When storms rage fiercely, and skies turn gray,
Remember the sun will rise another day.
With each new dawn, a chance to renew,
To find the strength within, to start anew.

Embrace the challenges that come your way,
For they shape your spirit, come what may.
In every setback, a lesson to learn,
To rise above, and let your soul yearn.

Believe in yourself, trust in your might,
You're capable of reaching any height.
Banish the doubts that cloud your mind,
And let your dreams, like stars, align.

Surround yourself with love and light,
And let kindness guide you, day and night.
With open arms, embrace the unknown,
And watch your spirit beautifully grown.

Together we stand, united and strong,
Lifting each other when things go wrong.
For in unity, we find the power to heal,
To uplift, inspire, and make hearts feel.

So let your spirit soar, like a bird in flight,
Embrace the joy, and let your soul take flight.
You are worthy, deserving of all that's good,
Embrace the journey and live as you should.

In this uplifting dance of life we share,
May hope and love be always there.
For in the darkest times, light will prevail,
And in our hearts, an uplifting tale.

Selfishness

In a world consumed by selfish desires,
Where compassion wanes and empathy tires,
There lies a darkness, deep and wide,
Where self-centeredness becomes our guide.

In the pursuit of personal gain,
We trample hearts, causing endless pain.
Blinded by our wants, we fail to see,
The damage we inflict, how it shouldn't be.

Selfishness breeds a lonely existence,
A life devoid of true, heartfelt assistance.
We build walls around our hearts and souls,
Neglecting the power to make others whole.

But let us pause, and take a moment to reflect,
On the consequences of our neglect.
For in our selfish pursuits, we lose sight,
Of the beauty found in selfless light.

True joy lies not in what we amass,
But in the love we give, the bonds that last.
A kind gesture, a helping hand,
Can bring solace to a troubled land.

Let us break free from this selfish grip,
And embrace compassion, let our hearts equip.
For in giving selflessly, we find release,
And fill our lives with purpose and peace.

Reach out to others, lend an ear,
Offer support, wipe away a tear.
In acts of selflessness, we find our worth,
And create a world of harmony and mirth.

So let us shed the cloak of selfishness away,
And let kindness and empathy lead the way.
For in a world where selflessness prevails,
We'll find the love and unity that never fails.

Disliked

In the realm of tastes, opinions sway,
Not all flavors suit us, that's okay.
For in the world of varied views,
Disliked things can still hold value and hues.

Like a canvas painted with diverse strokes,
Disliked things challenge our personal yokes.
They teach us lessons, broaden our sight,
And offer perspectives, both dark and light.

A song that grates upon our ears,
May bring joy to someone else, it appears.
The beauty lies in diversity's embrace,
Where different tastes find their own space.

Disliked books may hold a hidden gem,
A story waiting to resonate within.
For what one finds dull, another finds profound,
In the realm of art, such wonders abound.

Disliked moments, though they may cause strife,
Can shape our character, expand our life.
They test our patience, resilience, and grace,
And help us grow at our own pace.

Disliked can be a spark for change,
A catalyst to question, rearrange.
For in the discomfort of what we shun,
New insights and growth can be won.

83

So let us honor dislikes, without disdain,
Recognizing the power they contain.
They remind us of our unique identity,
And fuel the pursuit of what sets us free.

In this tapestry of likes and dislikes we weave,
Let's respect the diversity, and believe,
That what we dislike has its own worth,
For in the contrasts, we find our rebirth.

Bad guys love

In the realm of love's intricate dance,
A tale unfolds of a girl entranced.
She fell for a man, captivating and sly,
Unaware of the darkness hidden in his eye.

His words like honey, so sweet and smooth,
Wrapped around her heart, she couldn't remove.
She thought she found love in his charming
guise,
But little did she know, it was all a disguise.

He played with her emotions, a master of deceit,
Toying with her trust, making her feel
incomplete.
He reveled in her vulnerability and pain,
Leaving scars on her heart, like an indelible
stain.

She believed his promises, his vows of forever,
But they were empty words, meant to sever.
He broke her spirit, shattered her dreams,
Leaving her lost in a world of silent screams.

Yet within the darkness, a flicker of light,
A strength awakened, burning bright.
She found the courage to break free from his
hold,
To reclaim her worth, to be strong and bold.

She learned a painful lesson, through tears and
cries,
That a bad guy's love is built upon lies.
She vowed to seek out a love pure and true,
One that would cherish and honor her too.

For a girl's true love should uplift and heal,
A love that's genuine, honest, and real.
She'll find a partner who sees her worth,
And together they'll create a love that's rebirth.

So let her heart mend from the bad guy's sting,
As she spreads her wings, ready to take to the
sky.
For in her journey of love, she'll come to find,
A love that's deserving, gentle, and kind.

Work like a slave but eat like a king

Through toil and sweat, day after day,
I work like a slave, I don't dismay.
From dawn till dusk, my efforts persist,
In pursuit of a dream, a life blissed.

With hands calloused and muscles strained,
I labor relentlessly, undeterred, unchained.
For hard work is the path I tread,
To carve my destiny, where dreams are fed.

I sow the seeds, tend to the soil,
With unwavering dedication, I toil.
Through seasons of struggle, harvests of gain,
I cultivate my future, amidst sun and rain.

Though the road may be rugged and steep,
I persevere, for the rewards run deep.
For in the fields of labor, I seek not in vain,
To harvest abundance, to ease every strain.

And when the day is done, weary and worn,
I sit at my table, where joy is reborn.
For I eat like a king, with gratitude's feast,
Savoring the fruits of my tireless beast.

A meal earned through the sweat on my brow,
A testament to the work I endow.
In each bite savored, I taste victory's song,
Knowing my efforts have made me strong.

For work like a slave, but eat like a king,
Is the mantra that drives me, that makes my
heart sing.
In the balance of labor and reward, I find my
stride,
A life of purpose, where dreams coincide.

So I'll continue to work with unwavering might,
Knowing that my labor will yield delight.
For in the cycle of effort and reward, I'll bring,
A life where I work like a slave, but eat like a
king.

I apologize for loving you so much

In the depths of my heart, I find remorse,
A weight upon my soul, a lingering force.
For I apologize for loving you so much,
For letting my emotions have such a powerful
touch.

In the realm of love, I lost my way,
Allowing my heart to lead, come what may.
But in my affection, I overwhelmed your heart,
A burden too heavy, tearing us apart.

I apologize for the tears I caused to fall,
For the moments of despair, the shattered wall.
My love, though genuine, became a storm,
Engulfing us both, in its relentless form.

I apologize for the times I smothered your space,
For not giving you the freedom and grace.
Love should be a gentle, nurturing embrace,
Not a prison that confines, leaving no trace.

In my passion, I failed to see,
That love should be balanced, allowing us to be
free.
I apologize for the mistakes I made,
For the pain I inflicted, the price we paid.

But from this lesson, I've learned and grown,
To cherish boundaries, to make them known.
Love should be a dance, a harmonious blend,

Where both hearts soar, and both hearts mend.

So I apologize for the love that was too much,
For not understanding the delicate touch.
I'll strive to love with wisdom and care,
Respecting your space, and the love we share.

For in forgiveness and growth, we'll find our
way,
To a love that's stronger, come what may.
I apologize, my love, for the past's heavy clutch,
And promise to love you with a lighter touch.

Paulette my love

In the realm of words and rhymes,
Where love's essence forever chimes,
I write this verse for you, Paulette,
A tribute to the love we've met.

Paulette, my love, a shining star,
Guiding me, no matter how far,
Your presence fills my every day,
With warmth and love in every way.

Your smile, a beacon in the night,
A source of joy, pure and bright,
It lights up my world, my dear,
Erasing all shadows, removing fear.

Your laughter, like a melody divine,
Echoes through my heart, entwined,
Bringing solace to my weary soul,
Making me feel complete and whole.

In your eyes, I see a universe unfold,
A story of love that will never grow old,
With every glance, my heart takes flight,
Lost in the depths of your love's light.

Together we've weathered storms and strife,
Hand in hand, embracing this precious life,
Through highs and lows, thick and thin,
Our love remains, an unbreakable kin.

Paulette, my love, my heart's desire,
You fuel the flames of passion's fire,
With you, my love, I've found my home,
A love that's boundless, forever to roam.

So, let this poem be an eternal vow,
To cherish and love you, then and now,
For you, Paulette, are my everything,
A love that makes my heart sing.

In love with you

In the depths of my heart, a fire burns,
A love so profound, my soul yearns,
For you, my darling, are the light I see,
The center of my world, the key to me.

From the moment our eyes first met,
A love so sweet, I'll never forget,
You became the melody in my song,
The inspiration that makes me strong.

Every day, my love for you grows,
Like a gentle breeze that warmly flows,
It wraps around us, like a tender embrace,
Filling our lives with passion and grace.

Your smile, like sunshine on a cloudy day,
Melts away my worries, takes them away,
In your laughter, I find pure delight,
A symphony of joy, a beautiful sight.

Your touch, a spark that ignites my soul,
Sending shivers through me, making me whole,
With every caress, my heart skips a beat,
Lost in a love that feels so sweet.

In your eyes, I find a universe untold,
A love story that never grows old,
They mirror the love that dwells in me,
A love that's boundless, wild and free.

So here I stand, with words sincere,
In this poem, my love, I hold you dear,
Forever and always, my heart is true,
For I am deeply in love with you.

Fallin for you

As seasons change and colors blend,
A tale of love begins to transcend,
With every beat, my heart takes flight,
For in your presence, it feels so right.

Like autumn leaves, I gently fall,
Captivated by your mesmerizing call,
Your voice, a melody, enchanting and pure,
Leaving me craving for more and more.

In your eyes, I see a twinkling star,
Guiding me through, no matter how far,
They hold a depth, a captivating gaze,
Drawing me closer, in a love-filled haze.

Your laughter dances upon the air,
A symphony that erases all despair,
Its joyful notes, a soothing balm,
Wrapping me in a love-filled calm.

The touch of your hand, a gentle caress,
Leaves an imprint, a feeling I confess,
It sets my heart aflame, a burning desire,
Igniting a love that will never tire.

With every word you say, every smile you share,
I find myself falling, without a care,
Into a love so tender, so pure and true,
I'm falling for you, there's nothing I can do.

You've captured my heart, my soul, my all,
I'm grateful for this love, so vast and tall,
Together we'll journey, hand in hand,
In a love story that's beautifully grand.

So here I stand, with emotions profound,
In this poem, my love, I am spellbound,
For I have fallen, completely and true,
Head over heels, deeply in love with you.

Emotional damage

Within the depths of a wounded heart,
Lies the tale of emotional damage, a painful art.
Scars unseen, but etched deep within,
A reminder of battles fought, where hurt had
been.

Emotional damage, like a tempest's wrath,
Leaves a trail of brokenness in its path.
Words spoken with malice, actions unkind,
Leaving fragile souls shattered, confined.

The wounds may heal, but the marks remain,
A constant reminder of the lingering pain.
Trust, once vibrant, now fragile and worn,
Takes time and care to be reborn.

Yet, amidst the darkness that damage brings,
There's strength in resilience and growth that
springs.
Emotions tempered by lessons learned,
Wisdom gained from the bridges burned.

With time, healing finds its gentle way,
Like a soothing rain on a summer's day.
Love and compassion, the balm that soothes,
Mending the fractures, filling the bruise.

Emotional damage, a battle scar,
Doesn't define who you truly are.
For within your spirit, a flame still burns,

A resilient heart that longs to learn.

So embrace your journey, tender and true,
Acknowledge the pain, but let it not define you.
Let love and self-care be your guiding light,
Rebuilding your spirit, shining ever so bright.

For in the face of emotional damage, my dear,
You possess the strength to persevere.
You are resilient, courageous, and strong,
And from the ashes, a new melody will emerge, a
song.

Karma

In the realm of life's intricate dance,
There exists a force, a cosmic balance,
It's called Karma, a universal law,
Guiding our actions, with its unwavering jaw.

Like a boomerang, it returns what we sow,
Reaping the seeds we've let go,
The choices we make, the deeds we impart,
Shape our destiny, etching them in our heart.

For every act of kindness, a ripple is sent,
Touching lives, spreading love, heaven-sent,
The energy we share, the love we impart,
Karma reflects them back, a work of art.

But beware, for negative deeds have a cost,
Their consequences felt, never to be lost,
The pain we inflict, the harm we cause,
Karma's watchful eye, it never pauses.

It teaches us lessons, both gentle and tough,
To learn from mistakes, to rise when we've
sloughed,
To cultivate empathy, compassion, and grace,
To tread on this Earth with love in our embrace.

Karma holds us accountable, in every aspect,
The choices we make, the paths we select,
It reminds us that we are connected, intertwined,
That our actions ripple through space and time.

So let us strive for goodness, for light,
To live with integrity, both day and night,
For Karma is a mirror, reflecting our soul,
A reminder to align our purpose, to make us
whole.

In the grand tapestry of life's grand scheme,
Karma weaves its threads, like a timeless dream,
Embrace its teachings, let love be your guide,
And in harmony with the universe, may you
reside.

Knowing you worth

In the vast realm of self-discovery,

A journey unfolds, a profound odyssey,
To know your worth, deep within your core,
Unveiling the treasures you've yet to explore.

For you, my dear, are a unique soul,
With qualities that make you whole,
A tapestry woven with colors bright,
A beacon of light in the darkest night.

Know your worth, like a precious gem,
A radiant light that can't be condemned,
Embrace your strengths, your talents, your grace,
And let them shine in every space.

Release the doubts that weigh you down,
For within you lies a majestic crown,
You're worthy of love, respect, and more,
A treasure to be cherished, down to the core.

Value your heart, your dreams, and desires,
Ignite the flame of passion that never tires,
Believe in yourself, with unwavering faith,
And conquer the challenges you'll face.

In a world that may try to dim your light,
Stand tall and shine, with all your might,
Embrace your uniqueness, let it unfurl,
For you, my dear, are a precious pearl.

Remember, worth is not defined by another,
It resides within you, like a hidden treasure,
Embrace your worth, it's a priceless gift,
And let it uplift your spirit and spirit.

So, know your worth, embrace it strong,
Let it guide you, as you journey along,
You are worthy of love, happiness, and more,
A radiant soul that the world can't ignore.

Feeling worthless

In the depths of despair, I find myself lost,

Aching echoes of a heart that's been tossed,
A poem of anguish, a tale of worthlessness,
A soul burdened by darkness, seeking solace.

Amidst the shadows, my spirit does falter,
Whispers of doubt, they begin to alter,
The belief in myself, once strong and true,
Now shrouded in a haze, feeling so blue.

I walk through the world, a ghost in disguise,
A hollow vessel, devoid of light in my eyes,
The weight of worthlessness, heavy on my chest,
A constant reminder, I'm not like the rest.

But let me tell you, dear friend of mine,
In these moments of darkness, stars still shine,
For within your being, a spark does reside,
A flicker of brilliance, waiting to be revived.

You are not defined by the doubts you hold,
Nor the worthlessness that's taken its toll,
You're a tapestry of stories, a masterpiece
untold,
A symphony of emotions, waiting to unfold.

Embrace your imperfections, your scars and your
flaws,
For they shape your journey, and give you pause,
Know that you matter, in ways yet unseen,

You're a universe of wonder, a soul so serene.

When you feel worthless, remember this truth,
You're a priceless treasure, filled with infinite
youth,
Find strength in your struggles, and courage to
rise,
For within your heart, your worth never dies.

So hold your head high, and dry those tears,
You're worthy of love, and conquering fears,
Embrace your worth, and let your light gleam,
For you are extraordinary, a beautiful dream.

Life goes on

In the tapestry of time, life weaves its song,
A symphony of moments, both short and long,
Through joy and sorrow, it dances along,
With each passing day, life goes on.

When the sun rises high, painting the sky,
Or when storm clouds gather, and tears fill your
eye,
Through seasons of change, and moments gone
by,
Life keeps moving forward, with a gentle sigh.

In the depths of despair, when darkness
surrounds,
When hope seems fleeting, and solace is seldom
found,
Remember, dear soul, as the world spins around,
Life's ceaseless rhythm will once again astound.

For in every ending, a new beginning awaits,
A chance to grow stronger, to change our fates,
The cycle of life, like a river that navigates,
Through twists and turns, it never hesitates.

With every sunrise, there's a chance to restart,
To mend broken pieces and heal a wounded
heart,
To embrace the unknown, and play your part,
For life goes on, a masterpiece of art.

So cherish each moment, both big and small,
For life's precious gift is meant to enthrall,
Embrace the laughter, and embrace the fall,
For in this grand journey, you'll find it all.

Through triumphs and failures, you'll learn to be
strong,
To dance through the melodies, embracing the
throng,
In the ebb and flow of life's endless song,
Remember, my friend, life indeed goes on.

Shadow

In the realm where light meets darkness'
embrace,
There exists a presence, a mysterious grace,
It follows our steps, ever silent and near,
A loyal companion, our shadow, so clear.

In the sun's golden rays or the moon's gentle
glow,
Our shadow dances, wherever we may go,
A silhouette of secrets, it faithfully reflects,
The depths of our being, our hidden aspects.

When we stand tall, it stretches far and wide,
A companion that lingers, forever by our side,
In moments of triumph, it grows tall and proud,
A testament to strength, it whispers aloud.

Yet in times of despair, it may seem to grow,
Engulfing our souls, casting a darkened shadow,
But fear not, dear friend, for shadows can't
prevail,
They merely remind us of the light's delicate
tale.

For within every shadow, there's a flicker of
light,
A reminder that darkness can't conquer the
fight,
It takes both the sun and the moon to dance,
To create the beauty of life's cosmic expanse.

So embrace your shadow, both light and shade,
For it's a part of you, an intricate braid,
It teaches us balance, it teaches us grace,
In the duality of life, it finds its rightful place.

In the tapestry of existence, shadows play their
role,
They deepen our understanding, they make us
whole,
So let us befriend them, these companions
unseen,
For in their depths, our true selves are gleaned.

Embrace your shadow, with love and with care,
For it mirrors your journey, the burdens you
bear,
In unity and acceptance, we find our release,
For shadows, like life, bring us moments of
peace.

Don't hurt me

In a world of scars and tender hearts,

Where pain and sorrow tear us apart,
I raise my voice, with a plea so sincere,
Don't hurt me, dear world, let compassion
appear.

For the wounds we bear, both seen and unseen,
Are etched on our souls, where love once had
been,
We long for solace, a respite from strife,
A sanctuary where we can heal and find life.

In the depths of despair, we seek refuge and
peace,
A sanctuary where our fears can finally cease,
Let kindness be the compass that guides our
way,
And empathy the language we speak every day.

Don't hurt me with words, sharp as a knife,
For they carve scars deep within, affecting my
life,
Choose instead gentle words, that uplift and
inspire,
To ignite a flame of hope, extinguishing the fire.

Don't hurt me with actions, harsh and unkind,
For they shatter my spirit, leaving wounds
behind,
Extend a helping hand, a gesture of care,

To remind me that love and compassion are
there.

Let us build a world, where hurt finds no place,
Where understanding and love interlace,
For in unity and kindness, we find strength
anew,
Creating a haven where dreams can come true.

So embrace me with tenderness, with open arms,
Let compassion and empathy be our guiding
charms,
In a world that's hurting, let's choose a different
way,
To heal, to uplift, and to make darkness sway.

Don't hurt me, dear world, let's join hands and
see,
The power of love and its ability to set us free,
Together we can rise, above pain and strife,
Embracing a world where we cherish each other's
life.

You're my favorite

In the realm of favorites, where passions reside,
There's a special place where hearts confide,
A cherished realm, where memories unfold,
A tapestry of treasures, both new and old.

A favorite song, that stirs the soul,
With lyrics that resonate, making us whole,
Its melody dances, through every beat,
A symphony of emotions, so bittersweet.

A favorite book, with pages well-worn,
Each chapter a journey, where dreams are born,
Its words like magic, transporting our mind,
To realms of wonder, where worlds intertwine.

A favorite place, where serenity prevails,
A sanctuary where the heart unfurls and sails,
Whether by the ocean or beneath starlit skies,
This sacred haven brings joy to our eyes.

A favorite moment, etched in our hearts,
A memory that time cannot tear apart,
A laughter shared, a touch so dear,
A connection that lingers, year after year.

But amidst these favorites, there's one that shines,
Above all others, it intertwines,
For in your presence, I find my delight,

You, dear friend, are my favorite, day and night.

Your smile, a beacon that lights up my day,
Your laughter, a melody that leads the way,
Your kindness, a treasure that warms my soul,
You're my favorite, making me feel whole.

Poisons

In shadows deep where darkness dwells,

A tale of poison, its story tells.
A venomous curse, a deadly brew,
Unleashing grief, its victims slew.

Beware the whispers of the serpent's tongue,
Its venomous words, a luring song.
Entangled in deceit, the naive heart,
The poison's dance tears worlds apart.

Its tendrils slither, silent and sly,
Corrupting hearts with a wicked lie.
With every drop that taints the soul,
A poison's grip takes full control.

In poisoned veins, a wildfire spreads,
Consuming love, where hope once tread.
The sweetest nectar, now laced with gall,
A treacherous elixir, to make one fall.

Oh, poison's kiss, so cruel and sly,
A siren's touch, a wicked lie.
It weaves its web, a lethal embrace,
Leaving sorrow in its poisonous trace.

But in the darkness, a light will gleam,
A remedy to shatter the poison's scheme.
Love's antidote, a balm so pure,
Healing wounds that poison once ensured.

So let us guard our hearts with care,
From poison's touch, its deadly snare.
For in our souls, resilience blooms,
And love's embrace dispels the gloom.

Let us be wary, yet steadfast and strong,
Defying poison's call, refusing its song.

Beautiful lady

Where elegance abounds,
There walks a lady, a beauty that astounds.
Her presence, a painting, a masterpiece divine,
A symphony of grace, a sight so fine.

Her eyes, like glistening pools of deepest blue,
Hold secrets and dreams, enchanting and true.
They speak volumes, in whispers soft and sweet,
Revealing a soul that's gentle and complete.

Her smile, a radiant sunbeam in the morn,
Lights up the world, where shadows are torn.
It dances upon her lips, a melody so rare,
Unveiling a joy that's beyond compare.

Her laughter, a melody, a blissful refrain,
Like songbirds in harmony, a delightful chain.
With every sound, it lifts spirits high,
Filling hearts with mirth, touching the sky.

Her touch, a feather's caress, so tender and light,
Brings solace and warmth, dispelling the night.
With gentle grace, her hands weave magic's spell,
Healing wounds, making broken hearts swell.

But beauty lies not in mere outward appeal,
It dwells within, where authenticity is real.
Her kindness, compassion, and love's sweet
embrace,
Are the truest forms of beauty, full of grace.

115

For a beautiful lady is more than just face,
It's the radiance of her soul, her inner space.
With strength and wisdom, she lights up the
way,
Guiding others with love, each and every day.

So let us celebrate the beauty she beholds,
The way she inspires, the stories she unfolds.

You broke me first

In the shattered fragments of a broken heart,

Lies a tale of pain, where love fell apart.
You broke me first, with your callous touch,
Leaving scars that ache, hurting so much.

Like fragile glass, my trust, it shattered,
As your words pierced through, leaving me
battered.
In the depths of despair, I drowned in sorrow,
Lost in the echoes of a love that's hollow.

You played with fire, with no regard,
Igniting flames that left my soul scarred.
Promises whispered, now turned to dust,
Leaving me questioning, lost in mistrust.

You broke me first, but I'll rise anew,
From the ashes of heartbreak, I'll renew.
For in pain's embrace, strength finds its birth,
And resilience emerges from the depths of
dearth.

I'll gather the pieces, mend what's been torn,
For in healing's journey, I shall be reborn.
With time as my ally, I'll find my way,
And the wounds you inflicted will fade away.

Though you broke me first, I'll reclaim my might,
Embracing the darkness, I'll seek the light.
For a shattered heart, with time, will heal,

And in the process, a stronger soul reveals.

So thank you, for the pain and the strife,
For through it all, I'll rebuild my life.
You broke me first, but I'll rise above,
Stronger, wiser, and filled with self-love.

Gamer

In the realm of screens and digital might,

Where worlds come alive in vibrant light,
There dwells a gamer, a hero in disguise,
Mastering realms where imagination flies.

With nimble fingers and eyes so keen,
They navigate worlds yet to be seen.
In virtual realms, they embark on quests,
Unleashing their skills, putting them to the test.

They wield controllers, their weapons of choice,
Guiding avatars with a confident voice.
In pixelated lands, they conquer and explore,
Unleashing their spirit, forever seeking more.

They climb mountains and sail through the sky,
Defying gravity, where limits don't apply.
They solve puzzles, unravel mysteries unknown,
Writing their story, in games they've grown.

In multiplayer realms, they join forces strong,
Building alliances, where friendships belong.
Together they triumph, united as one,
Bound by a passion that cannot be undone.

From pixels and sprites, narratives unfold,
With every achievement, their stories are told.
Their dedication fuels the digital fire,
For gaming is more than the games they acquire.

It's a journey of discovery, a world to explore,
A canvas for dreams, where legends soar.
With each game played, they find a new part,
A reflection of themselves, an extension of heart.

So hail the gamer, the warrior within,
Whose spirit ignites, where adventures begin.
In their hands, controllers, and keyboards they
hold,
A passion for gaming, a story yet untold.

Car

In a world of asphalt and endless miles,
My faithful steed, my car, brings me smiles.
Its metal frame, a vessel of might,
Through winding roads, it carries my light.

With polished curves and gleaming sheen,
A beauty on wheels, a sight unseen.
Its engine roars, a symphony of power,
As we glide through the hours, minute by hour.

Oh, my dear car, with tires that grip,
You navigate the roads with an agile skip.
From countryside lanes to bustling streets,
You take me on journeys, where my heart beats.

From morning commutes to late-night drives,
You're a haven of solace, where freedom thrives.
With windows down and wind in my hair,
I feel alive, without a single care.

Through seasons of rain and sunlit days,
You're my companion, in so many ways.
With each journey shared, memories unfold,
Etched in my heart, never to grow old.

You carry me to new places afar,
A symbol of freedom, my guiding star.
Oh, my beloved car, a friend so true,
I'm grateful for the adventures we pursue.

So let's keep rolling, on roads unknown,
Exploring the world, with you I'm not alone.
Together we'll conquer every distant shore,
In my car, I find joy, forevermore.

Drinking

In amber glasses, liquid gold,
A tale unfolds, as stories are told.
Within the depths of swirling streams,
A symphony of flavors, a poet's dreams.

A toast to life, to moments shared,
To laughter ringing, without a care.
In glasses raised, in camaraderie,
We find solace, in joyful revelry.

From sparkling wines to aged whiskey,
Each sip unlocks a realm so risky.
In swirling spirits, whispers reside,
Unleashing truths we often hide.

In bars and taverns, our hearts unwind,
Drinks of courage, a gentle kind.
With each libation, inhibitions fade,
A dance of mirth, where worries wade.

But beware the allure of the liquid fire,
For it can consume, and desires inspire.
In moderation, find the sweet embrace,
Lest the elixir become a perilous chase.

For in the depth of a well-crafted brew,
Lies the power to heal, to bond, to renew.
To celebrate life's triumphs and sorrows,
To chase away shadows with brighter
tomorrows.

So let us raise our glasses high,
To nights of laughter 'neath starry sky.
In the company of friends, old and new,
Here's to drinking, to moments true.

Infidelity

In shadows cast upon a love once pure,
Lies a tale of betrayal, hearts unsure.
A solemn dance of secrets, whispered low,
Infidelity's web, where trust lays low.

In the sanctuary of vows once sworn,
A crack forms, where doubts are born.
A fleeting glance, a stolen touch,
The fire of temptation, it burns too much.

Oh, the agony of a love undone,
When loyalty falters, hearts come undone.
A web of deceit, a tangled affair,
Leaving hearts shattered, beyond repair.

From whispered promises to hidden lies,
The truth obscured, behind veiled eyes.
A web of pain, where hearts entwined,
Yet, in the darkness, love is undermined.

For infidelity breeds a bitter taste,
A poison that spreads with reckless haste.
It tears apart the fabric of trust,
Leaving scars on hearts, forever unjust.

But let us not forget the path to heal,
To mend the wounds, to find what's real.
For forgiveness, though a daunting choice,
Can breathe new life, give broken hearts voice.

In the aftermath, lessons are learned,
From the embers of pain, growth is earned.
May love's journey guide us to the light,
And teach us to cherish, to do what's right.

Song of pain

(Verse 1)

In the depths of the night, a silent storm,

A battle within, where shadows swarm.
A heavy burden, a weight on the chest,
Depression's grip, it won't let me rest.

(Chorus)
Oh, depression, you're a cruel companion,
Stealing joy, leaving scars to deepen.
But I won't surrender, I'll find my way,
Through the darkest night, I'll see the day.

(Verse 2)
A clouded mind, a heart worn thin,
Lost in a maze, where hope grows dim.
But I'll keep fighting, though the road is tough,
Seeking solace, when the world feels rough.

(Chorus)
Oh, depression, you're a cruel companion,
Stealing joy, leaving scars to deepen.
But I won't surrender, I'll find my way,
Through the darkest night, I'll see the day.

(Bridge)
In the loneliness, I'll search for light,
Reaching out, breaking through the night.
With open arms, I'll embrace the pain,
For in the struggle, I'll rise again.

(Verse 3)
Though tears may fall, and darkness looms,
I'll gather strength, dispelling the gloom.
For in my heart, a flicker still burns,
A flame of resilience, it fiercely yearns.

(Chorus)
Oh, depression, you're a cruel companion,
Stealing joy, leaving scars to deepen.
But I won't surrender, I'll find my way,
Through the darkest night, I'll see the day.

(Outro)
So, I'll keep singing, this song of mine,
A testament to the strength I'll find.
In the depths of despair, I'll rise above,
With love and hope, I'll conquer, I'll love.

Song of broken heart

(Verse 1)

In the stillness of the night, I'm all alone,
A shattered heart, a love that's flown.
Memories linger, like whispers in the wind,
A broken melody, where do I begin?

(Chorus)
Oh, this broken heart, it's tearing me apart,
Shattered dreams, like fragments in the dark.
But I'll rise again, find the strength to mend,
With every beat, this heartache will transcend.

(Verse 2)
Once a flame burning bright, now it flickers low,
A love once cherished, lost in the undertow.
The echoes of laughter, now replaced by tears,
A broken heart, weighed down by fears.

(Chorus)
Oh, this broken heart, it's tearing me apart,
Shattered dreams, like fragments in the dark.
But I'll rise again, find the strength to mend,
With every beat, this heartache will transcend.

(Bridge)
Through the pain, I'll find my way,
Gathering the pieces, day by day.
I'll learn to heal, to love again,
And let the scars guide me, through the rain.

(Verse 3)
Though the road is long, and the nights are cold,
I'll find solace in the stories yet untold.
For a broken heart can mend, and love can
bloom,
In the midst of darkness, a new dawn will loom.

(Chorus)
Oh, this broken heart, it's tearing me apart,
Shattered dreams, like fragments in the dark.
But I'll rise again, find the strength to mend,
With every beat, this heartache will transcend.

(Outro)
So, I'll embrace the pain, and I'll let it go,
For a broken heart can still find its glow.
With time and grace, I'll find my way,
And love will guide me to a brighter day.

My wife

In a world where love's enchantment gleams,
There resides a queen within my dreams.
Her radiance eclipses the brightest star,
A love so pure, it knows no bizarre.

My pen shall paint her in poetic hues,
In verses that sing of her soul's muse.
Oh, how her eyes twinkle like the moonlit sea,
Reflecting the depths of her love for me.

Her smile, a sunrise breaking through the mist,
Ignites my heart with its tender twist.
Her laughter, like a symphony of delight,
Fills my days with joy, banishing the night.

Her touch, a gentle breeze against my skin,
Stirs a wildfire of passion deep within.
Her embrace, a haven where I find solace,
A sanctuary where I find eternal promise.

Her spirit, a lighthouse in the darkest storm,
Guiding me to safety, keeping me warm.
Her wisdom, a compass on life's winding road,
Leading me to happiness, lightening my load.

In her presence, time dances with delight,
As we weave a tapestry of love so bright.
Through life's trials, hand in hand we roam,
Bound by a love that makes our house a home.

So, here's to my wife, my heart's truest friend,
May our love's journey never see an end.
Forever grateful, my soul shall forever sing,
For in her arms, I've found my everything.

My privacy

In a world where screens and shadows collide,
Where boundaries erode, and secrets subside,
I seek refuge in the sacred realm of privacy,
A sanctuary where truth and solitude agree.

Amidst the noise and constant prying eyes,
I yearn for a space where my spirit can rise,
Where I can retreat, shielded from the crowd,
And in the silence, my thoughts are allowed.

Privacy, a fragile treasure to behold,
A cloak that shields the stories untold,
It grants us freedom to be our truest selves,
Away from judgment and society's swells.

In solitude's embrace, I find solace and peace,
A respite from the chaos, a moment's release,
A chance to reflect, to wander and explore,
To nurture the passions that my heart adores.

In privacy's sanctuary, dreams take flight,
Unfolding their wings in the still of the night,
Unburdened by scrutiny, they blossom and grow,
In the privacy's embrace, their beauty does show.

Yet, privacy's plight is now under duress,
As digital footprints leave trails of distress,
Our intimate moments on display, unmasked,
In a world where privacy is constantly tasked.

Let us not forget the importance it holds,
To protect our thoughts, our stories, untold,
For in privacy's sanctuary, we find our voice,
Our right to choose, our ability to rejoice.

So, let us safeguard this precious domain,
Where solitude and freedom forever remain,
Respecting the boundaries, embracing the plea,
For privacy, an essential gift, to truly be free.

Playing the fool, who thinks he's fooling me

In the masquerade of deceit, I see you play,
A fool's charade, in a cunning display.
But do not be fooled by your clever disguise,
For my eyes pierce through your intricate lies.

You dance and jest, with a practiced grace,
A master of deception, wearing a smiling face.
But beneath the mask, your intentions unravel,
A web of deceit, where truth begins to travel.

You think you deceive, with your silver tongue,
But your words, like whispers, come undone.
I see the glimmers of your hidden game,
A charade of shadows, fueled by hidden shame.

You think you're the puppeteer, pulling the
strings,
Manipulating perceptions, weaving false things.
But I am not blind to your cunning ways,
I see through the haze, where reality sways.

Your laughter echoes, a hollow sound,
As you parade as a jester, a fool renowned.
But in your jesting, the truth reveals,
The masks you wear, the secrets it conceals.

So play your game, with all your might,
But know that I see through the layers of night.
For the fool you think you're fooling, my friend,

Is a mirror reflecting your own pretense in the
end.

In this theater of shadows and disguise,
I stand as the audience, seeing through your lies.
No longer a victim, no longer a fool,
I see the truth, and I rise, resolute.

Smile

$\mathcal{A}$ smile, a wondrous work of art,
A gentle curve that warms the heart.
It speaks a language, sweet and true,
Transcending barriers, connecting me to you.

With lips upturned, a radiant glow,
A smile's enchantment begins to show.
It dances upon a face, like sunlight's gleam,
Chasing away shadows, bringing forth a dream.

A smile, a universal embrace,
A touch of magic upon a weary face.
It carries kindness and spreads delight,
A beacon of hope, a guiding light.

In moments of joy, it shines so bright,
Illuminating the world with pure delight.
It whispers of laughter and shared delight,
A symphony of happiness, a beautiful sight.

In times of sorrow, it offers solace,
A gentle reminder that we're not alone in this
race.
A smile can mend wounds, lift up the spirit,
Bring comfort within, help us to heal and lift.

A smile, a gift we all possess,
A simple act that can bring happiness.
So let it bloom upon your face,
And watch as it transforms time and space.

137

For a smile holds the power to ignite,
A chain reaction, spreading love and light.
So share your smile, let it be your art,
And watch as it touches every heart.

Heart attack a song of love

(Verse 1)

In the stillness of the night, the world fades
away,
A tale of love and pain, I'm here to convey,
A story of a moment that changed it all,
A sudden rush of fear, like a curtain call.

(Pre-Chorus)
It struck like lightning, a bolt from the blue,
A silent assassin, my heart it did pursue,
The rhythm of life, it stumbled and cracked,
A symphony disrupted, my soul under attack.

(Chorus)
Heart attack, oh, heart attack,
A battle of emotions, I can't hold back,
In the depths of my chest, the pain remains,
Heart attack, oh, heart attack, it's driving me
insane.

(Verse 2)
A whisper in the wind, a warning so faint,
I brushed it aside, thought it was a mistake,
But the tightening grip, the heaviness within,
It grew stronger, louder, like a siren's hymn.

(Pre-Chorus)
My breath grew shallow, my vision blurred,
A symphony of chaos, my world slowly stirred,

The clock ticking faster, as life flashed before my
eyes,
A moment of reckoning, a truth I can't disguise.

(Chorus)
Heart attack, oh, heart attack,
A battle of emotions, I can't hold back,
In the depths of my chest, the pain remains,
Heart attack, oh, heart attack, it's driving me
insane.

(Bridge)
But in the midst of darkness, a light did shine,
The hands of angels reaching out, a lifeline,
With every beat of hope, I found the strength,
To fight back, to heal, and go the extra length.

(Chorus)
Heart attack, oh, heart attack,
A battle of emotions, I can't hold back,
In the depths of my chest, the pain remains,
Heart attack, oh, heart attack, it's driving me
insane.

(Outro)
Now I stand here stronger, a survivor through
and through,
With each passing day, I cherish life anew,
So let this song be a reminder, a tale of rebirth,
That even in the darkness, love can heal the
earth.

I still love you though

In the depths of my heart, where emotions
reside,
A love remains unyielding, refusing to hide.
Through the storms and trials, it perseveres,
A flame that burns brightly, despite the years.

Though time may have passed, and seasons have
changed,
My love for you, dear, remains unarranged.
Through highs and lows, it has stood the test,
A love that's unwavering, forever blessed.

I still love you, though moments have flown,
Like whispers on the wind, our memories have
grown.
In the echoes of laughter and tears we've shed,
Our love's foundation, unbreakable, it's said.

Though distance may separate, our souls
intertwined,
Our hearts beat in rhythm, a connection defined.
Through the miles and miles of this world we
roam,
My love for you, darling, will always find home.

I still love you, through the passage of time,
Like an unending melody, a heartfelt rhyme.
In the silence of night, I feel your embrace,
A love that transcends, boundless in space.

Though life may unravel with its twists and
turns,
My love for you, sweetheart, forever burns.
In the tapestry of our story, woven with care,
I still love you, and I always will, I swear.

So let the stars bear witness to this eternal
flame,
As I whisper softly, and call out your name.
For in this vast universe, you're all I see,
My love for you, my dear, will forever be.

The beauty you can't see

In a world of shadows and hidden dreams,
There's a beauty that transcends what it seems.
I see the colors that paint the sky,
The miracles that make life worth the try.

I see the beauty you can't see,
Unveiling wonders for you and me.
In the delicate petals of a blooming flower,
Or the symphony of raindrops in a passing
shower.

I see the magic in a child's innocent gaze,
The spark of curiosity that forever stays.
In the laughter that dances upon the air,
And the love that binds hearts, so rare.

I see the beauty in a starry night,
Where wishes are born, taking flight.
In the gentle breeze that caresses your face,
And the sun's warm embrace, a loving embrace.

I see the beauty in the depths of your soul,
A tapestry of stories waiting to unfold.
In the strength that lies beneath your tears,
And the resilience that conquers all fears.

I see the beauty you can't perceive,
Within yourself, the power to believe.
In the scars that tell tales of battles fought,

And the lessons learned, the growth you've
sought.

So open your eyes, let the world unfurl,
Discover the beauty that makes your heart swirl.
For I see it clearly, a vision so grand,
The beauty that's woven through every strand.

I see the beauty you can't see,
A tapestry of life, a symphony set free.
Embrace it, my dear, and let your spirit soar,
For the beauty you can't see, forevermore.

Successful

There's a tale of triumph, a victorious stride.

A poem about success, let me paint the scene,
Of perseverance and glory, where dreams
convene.

Success is not a destination, but a journey
untold,
A path paved with determination, courageous
and bold.
It's the relentless pursuit of a meaningful goal,
The fire in your heart that fuels your soul.

Success is the sweat upon your brow,
The countless hours of work, you vow.
It's the resilience to rise after each fall,
And the unwavering belief that you can conquer
all.

Success is found in the lessons you learn,
The wisdom gained with every twist and turn.
It's the strength to embrace failure's sting,
And use it as a steppingstone to greater things.

Success is the joy of seeing your vision come
alive,
The satisfaction of knowing you've truly thrived.
It's the impact you make, the lives you touch,
And the legacy you leave, cherished so much.

But success is not measured in material gain,

Nor by the applause or the acclaim.
It's defined by the growth within your soul,
The person you become as you reach your goal.

So strive for success, but define it your way,
Let your passion guide you, day by day.
For success is a journey, unique to each soul,
A story of triumph that only you can unfold.

Wait don't leave

In the shadows of uncertainty, I stand,
With a plea in my heart, reaching for your hand.
A poem of longing, let my words convey,
The depths of my love, don't go away.

Wait, don't leave me, my soul's intertwined,
With yours, a connection, so deeply entwined.
In the echoes of laughter and tears we've shared,
The bond we've nurtured, a love that's rare.

In moments of weakness, you've been my
strength,
A guiding light, leading me through any length.
Your presence, a sanctuary, where I find peace,
With you by my side, all worries cease.

Wait, don't leave me, let's weather the storm,
Together, we're unbreakable, in any form.
In the tapestry of our story, we've grown,
Through trials and triumphs, we've always
known.

The memories we've woven, like threads in time,
A symphony of love, no words can define.
The laughter, the tears, the adventures we've
shared,
A portrait of a love that cannot be compared.

Wait, don't leave me, for my heart won't mend,
Without you, my love, it's a journey to no end.

In your eyes, I see a reflection of my soul,
A love so profound, it makes me whole.

Let's face the challenges, hand in hand,
Embracing the unknown, together we'll
withstand.
For our love is a flame that forever burns,
In the realm of eternity, our love returns.

Wait, don't leave me, let's create our destiny,
A future entwined, where our souls roam free.
With you by my side, I can conquer all,
For our love is a foundation, standing tall.

So stay, my love, let's weave our dreams,
In the tapestry of forever, where love redeems.
Wait, don't leave me, let's dance through the
night,
For without you, my love, everything loses its
light.

Love is a song

(Verse 1)

In a world where everything is changing,
Love remains the constant, never fading.
It's a feeling that's so profound,
It lifts you up when you're feeling down.

(Pre-Chorus)
Love, it's a fire that burns so deep,
A treasure that's yours to keep.
It's a melody that fills your soul,
Making you feel whole.

(Chorus)
Love, it's a symphony that never ends,
Two souls entwined, forever friends.
Through the highs and lows, we'll soar above,
This is a song about love.

(Verse 2)
Love is patient, love is kind,
It's a shelter from the storms we find.
It's a language that needs no words,
A bond that only true love affords.

(Pre-Chorus)
Love, it's a flame that lights the way,
Guiding us both night and day.
It's a feeling that's so divine,
In your arms, I find my rhyme.

(Chorus)
Love, it's a symphony that never ends,
Two souls entwined, forever friends.
Through the highs and lows, we'll soar above,
This is a song about love.

(Bridge)
Sometimes love can break your heart,
But it's worth the risk, right from the start.
For every tear that's ever been shed,
Love can heal and mend.

(Chorus)
Love, it's a symphony that never ends,
Two souls entwined, forever friends.
Through the highs and lows, we'll soar above,
This is a song about love.

(Outro)
So let the music play, let it ring,
Love is the song we'll forever sing.
Through the years, our hearts will dance,
In this eternal romance.

Six feet under

(Verse 1)

In the darkness, I'm drowning, lost my way,

Beneath the earth, where shadows tend to stay,
Six feet under, where my spirit's confined,
Yearning for a lifeline, a chance to rewind.

(Pre-Chorus)
Oh, I'm suffocating, trapped in this despair,
Searching for a savior, a glimmer of hope
somewhere,
Through the soil and the silence, I cry out for
release,
Will anyone hear me? Will someone bring me
peace?

(Chorus)
Save me from this grave, from the depths I can't
escape,
Break these chains that bind me, let me feel alive
again,
Pull me from the darkness, let the sunlight touch
my face,
Oh, I'm reaching out for you, won't you save me
from this place?

(Verse 2)
In this coffin of regrets, regrets that weigh me
down,
I'm haunted by memories that keep me bound,

But I'm pleading, I'm praying, for a chance to start anew,
To rise above the ashes, to find a love that's true.

(Pre-Chorus)
Oh, I'm suffocating, trapped in this despair,
Searching for a savior, a glimmer of hope somewhere,
Through the soil and the silence, I cry out for release,
Will anyone hear me? Will someone bring me peace?

(Chorus)
Save me from this grave, from the depths I can't escape,
Break these chains that bind me, let me feel alive again,
Pull me from the darkness, let the sunlight touch my face,
Oh, I'm reaching out for you, won't you save me from this place?

(Bridge)
I'm longing for salvation, for a chance to be reborn,
To break free from the darkness, to weather every storm,
I'll rise above the ashes, like a phoenix in the sky,
With your love as my guide, I'll no longer be denied.

(Chorus)
Save me from this grave, from the depths I can't escape,

Break these chains that bind me, let me feel alive
again,
Pull me from the darkness, let the sunlight touch
my face,
Oh, I'm reaching out for you, won't you save me
from this place?

(Outro)
Oh, save me, save me, from six feet under,
Let me breathe again, let my heart beat like
thunder,
In your arms, I'll find solace, I'll find my release,
Save me from this grave, and bring me back to
peace.

Burning Bridges

In the depths of my soul, a fire burns bright,

A blaze of fury, a destructive light,
For I have chosen to burn bridges behind,
Leaving naught but ashes, no path left to find.

Once upon a time, those bridges were strong,
Connecting hearts and souls, where we belonged,
But anger and resentment took their toll,
And now those bridges crumble, taking their
final role.

With every match struck, flames dance and rise,
Consuming the structure, severing ties,
The smoke billows high, as memories fade,
A painful reminder of the choices I've made.

Yet, in this conflagration, I find release,
A chance to let go, to find inner peace,
For those bridges, though burned, were built on
deceit,
And their charred remnants, a symbol of defeat.

But as the embers die down, my heart begins to
learn,
That burning bridges doesn't always mean I
yearn,
For a new path emerges, from the ashes it
springs,
A chance to rebuild, to grow new wings.

So, I'll embrace the lessons and the scars I've
gained,
From the bridges I burned, the bridges I stained,
And with newfound wisdom, I'll chart a new
course,
Forging connections stronger, with love as the
force.

For burning bridges, though drastic and severe,
Can pave the way for something bright and clear,
And as I move forward, leaving the past behind,
I'll build bridges anew, with a heart that's kind.

The Past Unchanged

In the depths of my thoughts, a haunting
refrain,
A reminder that echoes, causing me pain,
I yearn to rewrite what's etched in my past,
To undo the mistakes, to make them unlast.

But the past, like a river, forever will flow,
Its currents unyielding, no way to bestow,
Upon me the power to alter its course,
To rewrite the pages, to find a new source.

Oh, how I long to erase my regrets,
To mend broken bonds, to repay all my debts,
But time's cruel embrace holds memories tight,
And the past, once written, remains in plain
sight.

I cannot turn back the hands on the clock,
Or erase the footprints I left on the walk,
For the past is a teacher, a guide to the now,
A reminder of lessons that time won't allow.

Yet, in this acceptance, there lies a chance,
To grow and to learn, to rise from life's dance,
To shape a future with wisdom in hand,
To build upon ashes, where new dreams can
stand.

For the past is a canvas, painted in hue,
Of triumphs and failures, of joy and of rue,

And though I can't change what's engraved on its
face,
I can learn from its stories, find strength in its
grace.

So, I'll embrace the scars, the choices I've made,
For they've shaped who I am, the path that I've
laid,
And though I can't rewrite the chapters long
passed,
I'll create a new narrative, one that will last.

For in the tapestry of life, the past has its place,
A reminder to cherish each step, each embrace,
To live in the present, where moments are vast,
And find solace in knowing, the past is the past.

The Hero Within

In the depths of my being, a hero resides,
A warrior of courage, where strength collides,
For I am the protagonist, the star of my tale,
With the power to conquer, to prevail.

Through trials and tribulations, I rise above,
With unwavering spirit, fueled by love,
I am the hero, with a heart so bold,
Writing my story, as legends unfold.

In moments of darkness, I find the light,
I face my fears, ready to fight,
With determination, I break through the chains,
Defying the odds, where victory remains.

No longer a bystander, a passive role,
I take control, I'm the one in control,
For I am the hero, in charge of my fate,
Crafting my destiny, refusing to wait.

I face adversity with unwavering might,
Guided by virtue, with honor in sight,
Every obstacle becomes a stepping stone,
As I claim my power, no longer alone.

With every challenge, I discover my truth,
Resilient and steadfast, I stand as living proof,
That within me resides the strength to endure,
Writing my legacy, courageous and pure.

I am the hero of my own grand design,
Unleashing my potential, a force so divine,
The author of chapters, both triumph and strife,
Embracing my journey, embracing this life.

So, let the story unfold, let the battles be won,
For I am the hero, and my journey's just begun,
With purpose and passion, I'll conquer each test,
For I am the hero, and I'll be my very best.

Forever and for always

Forever and for always, our love shall endure,
A bond so unbreakable, strong and pure.
Through the trials of life, we'll stand side by
side,
In each other's arms, our spirits will reside.

Hand in hand, we'll brave the storms that arise,
With love as our compass, we'll reach the skies.
Through every sunset and dawn that we see,
We'll create a love story, just you and me.

In laughter and tears, in joy and in sorrow,
We'll face every challenge, today and tomorrow.
For our hearts are entwined, forever united,
In a love so profound, never to be blighted.

Through the passage of time, our love will grow,
Like a river that continuously flows.
With each passing day, our souls intertwined,
A love that's eternal, beautifully designed.

Our love will be a shelter in times of despair,
A beacon of hope when life seems unfair.
Through every season, in every endeavor,
Our love will remain strong, forever and ever.

With whispered words and gentle caress,
We'll cherish each moment, forever blessed.
In your embrace, I find solace and peace,
A love that transcends, never to cease.

Forever and for always, our spirits entwined,
In this cosmic dance, our souls aligned.
No distance or obstacle can keep us apart,
For our love is boundless, a work of art.

So, let us embrace this journey we share,
With a love so profound, beyond compare.
Forever and for always, our hearts will be true,
In this lifetime and beyond, I'll love only you.

I wish I never found you

I wish I never found you, my heart now torn,

For the love we shared has left me forlorn.
In the depths of regret, I drown in despair,
Wishing I could erase the moments we shared.

Your presence was a beacon, a captivating light,
But now it feels like a curse, a perpetual night.
The joy we once had has turned to sorrow,
Leaving me to wonder about a better tomorrow.

Oh, the pain of knowing what could have been,
If our paths had never crossed, if we had never
seen.
The happiness I thought I found in your
embrace,
Now a haunting memory I long to erase.

The echoes of your laughter still ring in my ears,
Reminding me of a time when love knew no
fears.
But now the laughter feels hollow and cold,
The warmth of your touch, a story untold.

I wish I never found you, to spare my heart the
ache,
To shield my soul from the wounds that won't
break.
But alas, the past cannot be rewritten or undone,
So I must learn to heal, to rise with the sun.

Though the pain may linger, I'll find my way,
To heal the wounds, to mend and to sway.
In time, I'll rebuild what was torn apart,
And find a love that mends this wounded heart.

So, I'll bid farewell to what could have been,
To the love that caused heartbreak within.
I'll carry the lessons, the scars that remain,
And grow stronger, despite the lingering pain.

For in the depths of darkness, I'll find my light,
And create a future that shines ever bright.
I wish I never found you, but I'll move on,
To a life where love and happiness are reborn.

Bad at love

I admit, I'm bad at love, it seems,
Caught in a cycle of shattered dreams.
A heart that falters, unsure and lost,
Paying the price for love's heavy cost.

I stumble through the dance of romance,
Tripping over my own insecurities, by chance.
Misreading cues, missing the signs,
Leaving love's sweet melody behind.

I struggle to open up, to let someone in,
Fearful of the pain that love may bring.
Guarding my heart, building walls so high,
Afraid to trust, afraid to try.

But deep down, there's a flicker of desire,
A longing to connect, to feel love's fire.
To find a love that's patient and kind,
A love that mends the scars I've left behind.

For being bad at love doesn't define me,
I'll learn from the past, set my heart free.
I'll embrace the flaws, the lessons learned,
And with a hopeful spirit, love will be returned.

I'll take my time, I'll tread with care,
Breaking the patterns that led to despair.
I'll grow and evolve, in love's sweet game,
Finding strength within, releasing the shame.

So, here's to the journey, the love yet to find,
To the battles fought and the ties that bind.
I may be bad at love, but I won't give in,
For one day, true love's victory I'll win.

Because you love me

In the depths of my heart, a love story blooms,

A tale of devotion that forever consumes,
With every breath, I feel your love's embrace,
And in your eyes, I find solace and grace.

Because you love me, the sun shines bright,
Each day is painted in hues of delight,
Your love's gentle touch, a soothing balm,
In your arms, I find a peaceful calm.

Because you love me, I am stronger each day,
Your unwavering support lights my way,
Through life's trials and storms, we stand tall,
Together we conquer, we never shall fall.

Because you love me, I believe in dreams,
The impossible becomes possible, it seems,
You inspire me to reach for the skies,
With you by my side, I can truly rise.

Because you love me, my spirit takes flight,
You lift me higher, beyond any height,
In your love's embrace, I find my home,
A sanctuary where my heart will always roam.

Because you love me, I am complete,
With you, my love, my heart finds its beat,
Forever grateful for the love we share,
Because you love me, life is beyond compare.

Lose you to love me

In shadows deep, where pain resides,
A heart once broken, wounded sides.
A tender soul, lost in the fray,
Searching for light to guide the way.

Through tear-filled nights and whispered cries,
A weary spirit seeks to rise.
Amidst the ache, a flicker of hope,
A chance to heal, to learn to cope.

Farewell to chains that held so tight,
To darkness veiled in endless night.
A choice emerges, brave and true,
To lose you, and find love anew.

For in the letting go, I find,
Strength to mend this heart of mine.
No longer tethered to your lies,
I spread my wings, embrace the skies.

With every shattered piece I find,
A stronger version, redefined.
From ashes born, a phoenix soars,
Reborn in love's eternal shores.

And as I walk this path alone,
I claim my worth, my heart's new home.
No longer bound by what we were,
I choose to love, to self-transfer.

For losing you was gaining me,
A chance to set my spirit free.
In tender grace, my heart does mend,
And in this love, my wounds transcend.

So let the past remain behind,
A distant memory, unconfined.
I rise above, I soar, I see,
The love I lost has set me free.

Scared to be lonely

In the depth of night, when shadows creep,

A heart whispers secrets, buried deep.
A soul yearning for love's tender embrace,
But haunted by the fear of an empty space.

Scared to be lonely, it cries in the dark,
Longing for a connection, a flame, a spark.
Yet walls are built, defenses so high,
To shield from the pain of a goodbye.

In crowds and chaos, it seeks a retreat,
Yearning for solace, a love that's complete.
But doubts and uncertainties play their part,
Tugging at the strings of a fragile heart.

The silence echoes, an eerie sound,
Aching for companionship, profound.
Yet fear holds sway, casting doubts and fears,
Creating a chasm, widening the tears.

But take heart, dear one, for love will find,
Its way to you, with gentle, patient kind.
For in vulnerability, strength does reside,
And in embracing solitude, love will abide.

Scared to be lonely, yet brave to explore,
The depths of your being, to the core.
In moments of solitude, a self is found,
A love that blossoms, unbound, unbound.

Let go of the fear, release the doubt,
Embrace the journey, both in and out.
For in the dance of solitude and connection,
A symphony of love finds its affection.

So don't be afraid to open your heart,
To embrace the beauty, the joy, and the art.
For in vulnerability, love takes flight,
Dispelling the darkness, bringing forth light.

Scared to be lonely, let courage be your guide,
For in the quest for love, you'll never be denied.
Embrace the unknown, step into the unknown,
And discover a love that's uniquely your own.

Angle of mine

Angel of mine, with wings so divine,

A celestial being, a presence sublime.
You grace my existence, with love untold,
Guiding me gently, through life's winding road.

Your eyes shine bright, like stars in the night,
Reflecting compassion, pure and bright.
Your touch is gentle, a soothing balm,
Healing my wounds with a love so calm.

In moments of darkness, you're my guiding light,
Guiding me through the depths of the night.
You lend me your strength when mine is frail,
Whispering words of hope when all seems to fail.

Your wings enfold me, in a comforting embrace,
Offering solace and a sense of grace.
You lift me up when I'm feeling low,
Nurturing my spirit, helping me grow.

Angel of mine, with a heart so pure,
You inspire me to be kind and endure.
You teach me the beauty of selfless giving,
And remind me of the joy of truly living.

In your presence, I find peace and serenity,
A divine connection, an everlasting unity.
You are my guardian, my source of light,
Guiding me through both day and night.

Angel of mine, I'm forever grateful,
For the love and guidance you faithfully dispel.
May your wings always carry you high,
As you watch over me with a vigilant eye.

Thank you, dear angel, for your unwavering care,
For being my ally, my solace, my prayer.
In this intricate dance of life, you're a sign,
That love and goodness are forever divine.

On my mind

In the depths of my thoughts, you reside,

A constant presence, my heart's guide.
In the corridors of my mind, you roam,
A cherished memory, a place called home.

You linger in the whispers of the breeze,
A melody playing through the trees.
In every moment, you're by my side,
A companion in this wild, life's ride.

You're a tapestry woven in my dreams,
A muse that ignites creative streams.
Your essence dances within my being,
A flame that keeps my soul from fleeing.

Thoughts of you paint colors so bright,
Illuminating even the darkest night.
Your laughter echoes like a sweet refrain,
Filling my world with joy and gain.

But sometimes, my mind becomes a storm,
With doubts and worries taking form.
In those moments, I seek solace in you,
A beacon of calm, a love so true.

On my mind, you leave an indelible trace,
A presence that time cannot erase.
In every thought, you find a place to reside,
A connection so deep, impossible to hide.

So here, within the confines of my mind,
You shall forever be enshrined.
A cherished memory, a love so kind,
Etched in the realms of my thoughts, entwined.

On my mind, you'll forever stay,
A constant presence, come what may.
In my heart, you'll always hold a space,
A love that time cannot erase.

One more try

Like a hidden treasure, buried deep,

My emotions awakened from a dormant sleep,
A love so profound, I couldn't foresee,
Enveloping my soul, setting me free.

In moments past, I couldn't comprehend,
The magnitude of love, a force that transcends,
But now I know, with every beat of my heart,
You're the missing piece, the essential part.

Through the ebbs and flows, the trials we face,
My love for you grows, at its own pace,
With each passing day, it becomes clear,
The depth of my affection, sincere and dear.

I didn't know how much I loved you,
Until I felt the absence, the void that grew,
You're the sun that shines in my darkest night,
Guiding me through, igniting my inner light.

Your smile, a beacon of hope and delight,
Your touch, a warmth that sets my soul alight,
Every word you speak, a melody divine,
With you by my side, life's colors brightly shine.

In your presence, I find solace and peace,
A love that brings me everlasting bliss,
I cherish each moment, each shared embrace,
For in your love, I've found my sacred place.

I didn't know how much I loved you,
But now I do, my heart's love so true,
Forevermore, I'll hold you close and near,
For my love for you, my dear, is crystal clear.

Song our time

(Verse 1)

In a world that's spinning, moving so fast,
I'm searching for a moment that will forever last,
Caught in the rhythm of life's endless race,
Yearning for a melody to find my inner space.

(Pre-Chorus)
I close my eyes, let the music take control,
A symphony of emotions, stirring in my soul,
I'll write a song that resonates with every heart,
A timeless anthem, where the magic will start.

(Chorus)
Oh, this is our time, let the music ignite,
Come together, unite, under a starry night,
With a melody that shines, and lyrics so true,
We'll sing it out loud, this hit song for me and
you.

(Verse 2)
In a world full of noise, I'll find the quiet,
Crafting a song that speaks of love's purest light,
From the depths of my heart, the words will
flow,
Capturing the moments that we've come to
know.

(Bridge)
We'll sway to the rhythm, lost in the sound,
A melody that echoes, all around,

With every note, we'll paint a vivid scene,
A song that captures dreams, like they've never
been.

(Chorus)
Oh, this is our time, let the music ignite,
Come together, unite, under a starry night,
With a melody that shines, and lyrics so true,
We'll sing it out loud, this hit song for me and
you.

(Verse 3)
In the chorus, we'll find our voices blend,
Singing words of hope that will never end,
A song that brings us closer, hand in hand,
Spreading love and joy across the land.

(Outro)
As the final chords fade into the night,
We'll hold this song, forever in our sight,
A hit that will soar, touching souls far and wide,
This song of ours, a timeless ride.

Hands up (song)

(Verse 1)

On a summer breeze, we're feeling alive,

Let's break free, let the rhythm drive,
The world is ours, no limits to explore,
We'll dance like wildfire, forevermore.

(Pre-Chorus)
Can you hear it in the air, the beat that's calling,
Our hearts are soaring, the energy enthralling,
With every step we take, the groove takes hold,
In this moment together, we're unstoppable,
bold.

(Chorus)
Hey, hey, let's lose control,
Feel the music deep within our souls,
Hands up high, we're gonna fly,
This catchy song will never die.

(Verse 2)
From the city streets to the neon lights,
We're chasing dreams, reaching new heights,
The bass is pumping, the crowd's on fire,
We're gonna set this night ablaze, take it higher.

(Pre-Chorus)
Can you feel the energy, electric in the air?
We're breaking barriers, we're a musical affair,
With every beat that drops, the vibe intensifies,
We'll keep on dancing, under starlit skies.

(Chorus)
Hey, hey, let's lose control,
Feel the music deep within our souls,
Hands up high, we're gonna fly,
This catchy song will never die.

(Bridge)
Oh, we're caught up in this melody,
Moving to the rhythm, wild and free,
The world disappears, we're in our own zone,
Together we're unstoppable, we've found our
home.

(Chorus)
Hey, hey, let's lose control,
Feel the music deep within our souls,
Hands up high, we're gonna fly,
This catchy song will never die.

(Outro)
As the night winds down, we'll carry the beat,
In our hearts, this song will forever repeat,
So let's sing it loud, and never say goodbye,
This catchy song, it's our anthem, reaching for
the sky.

Colors

You remind me of the colors, vibrant and bold,
A kaleidoscope of beauty, a story yet untold,
Each hue and shade, a glimpse into your soul,
A tapestry of emotions, that make me whole.

You're the red of passion, burning fierce and
bright,
Igniting flames within me, setting my heart
alight,
Like a blazing sunset, painting the sky with
desire,
Your presence kindles sparks, igniting a
passionate fire.

You're the blue of serenity, calm and serene,
A tranquil oasis, where I find peace within,
Like a peaceful ocean, stretching endlessly wide,
Your soothing presence, a refuge by my side.

You're the yellow of sunshine, radiating warmth
and cheer,
A beacon of light, when darkness draws near,
Like golden fields, dancing with gentle breeze,
Your smile brightens my world, puts my heart at
ease.

You're the green of nature, vibrant and alive,
Breathing life into my days, helping me thrive,
Like a lush forest, where dreams come to bloom,
Your nurturing spirit, dispelling any gloom.

You're the purple of mystery, enchanting and
wise,
A world of secrets, hidden within your eyes,
Like twilight's embrace, as the night draws near,
Your enigmatic presence, a treasure so dear.

You're the colors within me, a symphony of
grace,
A palette of emotions, that time can't erase,
With every shade you embody, a story to unfold,
You remind me of the colors, a masterpiece
untold.

Moment pass (Bring back love)

In the depths of our souls, where love resides,
Let us weave a tapestry, where hope abides.
For in this moment, where time stands still,
Let us rekindle love, let it be our thrill.

Don't let this moment pass, my dearest friend,
Bring back the love that knows no end.
In a world so vast, where darkness may creep,
Let our hearts entwine, the promises we keep.

With tender words and a gentle touch,
Let us mend the hurts that once were much.
For love is a flame that can never die,
It's a force that can lift us, reach the sky.

Don't let this moment pass us by,
With regret and longing, let love fly.
For in this fleeting dance, we find solace true,
A sanctuary of love, for me and for you.

Let's cast away the shadows that have grown,
And let our hearts embrace, as we've always
known.
For love is a gift, a treasure unbound,
Let it echo through time, with a melodious
sound.

Don't let this moment fade away,
Hold onto love, let it guide our way.
For in the beauty of love, we find our grace,

A symphony of souls, in a tender embrace.

So, my dear, let us seize this day,
Bring back the love that once held sway.
For in this fleeting moment, we have the power,
To create a love that will forever flower.

Don't let this moment pass, my love,
Let us rise, like the stars above.
For in our hearts, love will always reside,
A beacon of light, in which we confide.

Together we stand, hand in hand,
Defying the odds, as we understand,
That love is a choice, a conscious decision,
To bring back the love, with unwavering
precision.

So, let us not waste this precious time,
Let us reclaim love, make it truly shine.
For in this moment, where eternity lies,
We can bring back love, let it never demise.

Thousand miles

Oh, my, my, a thousand miles stretch wide,

Between you and I, on this journey we ride.
But fear not, my love, for distance can't sever,
The bond we share, it will last forever.

Though oceans may separate, and mountains
may rise,
Our hearts remain connected, under the same
skies.
For love knows no boundaries, no limits, no
bounds,
It transcends the miles, in whispers and sounds.

With every beat of my heart, it carries a plea,
To bridge the vast expanse, and bring you to me.
Through the miles we traverse, hand in hand,
A thousand miles apart, but united we stand.

In dreams, we'll meet, amidst moonlit shores,
Where time and space fade, and distance
restores.
For love is a flame that never ceases to burn,
A beacon of hope, a lesson to learn.

Oh, my, my, let's paint a celestial trail,
Across the midnight canvas, where stars prevail.
With each step we take, we'll close the divide,
A thousand miles between us, but love as our
guide.

In every whispered word, in every thought we
share,
We bridge the distance, showing how much we
care.
For love has no limits, it's a force so grand,
A thousand miles between us, but holding your
hand.

So, my love, let's embrace this bittersweet space,
Knowing that love can conquer any chase.
A thousand miles may seem like a lifetime away,
But our love will endure, come what may.

In the tapestry of time, we'll find our way
through,
A thousand miles apart, but forever me and you.
For distance is just a test, a trial we face,
But our love knows no bounds, it will always
embrace.

King in your story

I want to be the king in your story,

To reign with you in all your glory.
To unravel the secrets that lie within,
And discover the depths of who you've been.

Let me be the one to understand,
The intricacies of your heart's demand.
To peel back the layers, reveal your soul,
And together, create a tale untold.

I want to know the essence of your being,
The dreams you chase, the scars you're seeing.
To walk beside you, hand in hand,
Exploring the wonders of your wonderland.

In your eyes, I seek the truth,
The passion, the fire, the eternal youth.
Let us write our chapters, side by side,
Where love and adventure forever abide.

Tell me your fears, your hopes, your desires,
Set my soul ablaze with your inner fires.
For in your story, I long to play a part,
To hold your heart and never let it depart.

I want to be the one who knows your song,
The melodies that make your spirit strong.
To dance with you in the moonlit night,
And turn the ordinary into pure delight.

So, let me be the king in your story,
A partner, a lover, filled with love and glory.
Together we'll write a tale for the ages,
Where love prevails and passion engages.

And as we embark on this journey unknown,
Our hearts intertwined, forever grown,
I'll cherish the honor, the privilege, the art,
Of knowing the depths of your beautiful heart.

Kiss me through the phone

On a distant line, our connection is made,
A phone call that bridges the miles we've
strayed.
Through the airwaves, our voices entwined,
I yearn for your touch, your love so kind.

In whispered words, I hear your voice,
A symphony that makes my heart rejoice.
But oh, how I long for more than sound,
To feel your presence, to have you around.

So, kiss me through the phone, my love,
Let your affection descend from above.
Send your lips' warmth, your tender embrace,
Across the wires, filling this empty space.

Say you miss me, let the words take flight,
Through the receiver, like stars shining bright.
Let them wrap around me, like a gentle caress,
A reminder of the love we both confess.

Though distance separates our bodies apart,
Our souls remain entwined, bound by the heart.
In this phone call, we find solace and bliss,
A connection so strong, it's hard to dismiss.

But still, I yearn for the day we'll meet,
When distance is conquered, and love is
complete.
Until then, my love, let our words be true,

.Let them carry the passion that I have for you.

So, kiss me through the phone, my dear,
Let your love travel, loud and clear.
Say you miss me, with every breath you take,
Until the day we're together, love's own sake.

For in this phone call, a love story unfolds,
A testament to the love our hearts hold.
And until we're united, no longer apart,
I'll cherish each phone call, with all my heart.

Future, past and present

In the depths of time, where moments collide,
I am your future, your past, and your present,
side by side.
I exist in the echoes of what was and what will
be,
A symphony of existence, intertwined, you see.

In the tapestry of your life, I'm the thread that
weaves,
Connecting the chapters, the joys, and the
leaves.
I am the lessons learned, etched in your soul,
The experiences that shape you, helping you
grow.

As your future, I stand before you, a blank
canvas anew,
A realm of endless possibilities, waiting for you.
I hold the dreams and aspirations you hold dear,
Encouraging you to chase them without fear.

As your past, I reside in memories and time gone
by,
The footprints you've left, the tears you've cried.
I am the strength you've gathered from battles
fought,
The wisdom gained from lessons taught.

And as your present, I am here, right now,
The breath you take, the choices you allow.

I am the moment unfolding, the here and now,
Urging you to embrace the present, to take a
bow.

For I am the amalgamation of your journey's
embrace,
The culmination of experiences, creating your
space.
Past, present, and future, all intertwined,
Guiding you forward, with love undefined.

So, embrace me wholly, as I am your guide,
Your future, your past, and your present, side by
side.
For in the tapestry of time, we dance and we
sway,
Creating a legacy that will never fade away.

Prayers

In the silence of my soul's abode,
Where prayers take flight, in whispers sowed,
I find solace, a sacred embrace,
A refuge where hope finds its grace.

Like gentle rain on parched earth's skin,
Prayers descend, a soothing violin,
They carry my dreams on wings of light,
Guiding me through the darkest night.

In fervent words, my heart unfolds,
Its deepest longings, secrets untold,
Each syllable, a plea in disguise,
Seeking solace from heavenly skies.

Prayers are the songs of a troubled heart,
Seeking guidance, a brand new start,
They bridge the gap between here and above,
Connecting mortal souls with eternal love.

They weave a tapestry of faith and trust,
In the divine, in the infinite gust,
They transcend barriers, break every chain,
Uniting humanity in a harmonious refrain.

Prayers are whispers of gratitude's tune,
Expressions of love that forever bloom,
They carry our burdens, our fears they relieve,
Granting us strength to bravely believe.

In times of joy or in sorrow's embrace,
Prayers offer solace, a divine embrace,
They remind us of our fragile grace,
And the vastness of the cosmic space.

So, let us pray with open hearts,
With reverence, as each new day starts,
For in prayers, we find our truest voice,
And in their essence, we rejoice.

Water edges

*B*eneath the sky's expansive hue,

We sit by water, just me and you,
The gentle breeze whispers in our ears,
As we engage in conversations, void of fears.

In the ripples that dance upon the lake,
Our words find solace, no barriers to break,
We speak of dreams and passions untold,
Of stories written and secrets unfold.

Time slows down in this tranquil space,
As we ponder life's intricate embrace,
The water mirrors our thoughts so deep,
Reflecting the moments we choose to keep.

We share our joys, our laughter's sound,
And navigate the challenges we have found,
With every word, a new connection forms,
Like bridges built amidst life's storms.

The water listens, a patient friend,
As we talk of beginnings and journeys' end,
Of love's sweet embrace and hearts that mend,
In this sacred moment, we truly transcend.

We speak of hopes that paint tomorrow's dawn,
Of lessons learned from paths we've gone,
And as we converse, the world fades away,
Leaving us in a haven, where time holds sway.

By the water's edge, we find release,
A sanctuary of solace, a moment of peace,
Our voices intertwine, like a symphony's score,
As we unravel the mysteries we explore.

So let us sit here, by the water's edge,
Engaged in conversations, with words we pledge,
For in these moments, our spirits ignite,
And together, we embrace life's wondrous flight.

Scars

$\mathcal{I}$ could have shown you all the scars from the
start,
Bared my wounded soul, torn apart,
But vulnerability weighed heavy on my heart,
And that was always the most difficult part.

Each scar a story etched upon my skin,
A testament to battles fought within,
But sharing them meant the risk of judgment's
sting,
So I hid them away, beneath a guarded wing.

Those scars, they tell tales of trials and pain,
Of heartaches endured, and storms that left their
stain,
They speak of resilience, lessons hard-won,
Yet, baring them openly, I hadn't yet begun.

For scars reveal the battles fought in the dark,
The wounds that left their mark,
But they also hold the strength I've gained,
And the wisdom that remains.

I longed to open up, to let you see,
The depth of my journey, the real me,
Yet fear held me back, like a heavy chain,
Afraid of vulnerability's potential pain.

But now I realize, in hindsight's embrace,
That sharing my scars is an act of grace,

For in vulnerability, connections are formed,
And true understanding can be adorned.

So let me show you now, without any disguise,
The scars that speak of tears cried,
They're a part of me, woven into my art,
And revealing them was always the hardest part.

With courage, I'll unmask my hidden pain,
Embrace vulnerability, let trust regain,
For in the beauty of scars, I'll find my voice,
And let authenticity be my choice.

So, here I stand, ready to impart,
The stories etched within my heart,
For I've come to realize, and now impart,
That sharing scars is where healing truly starts.

Chaos and art

In the depths of my heart, a love takes hold,

For your soul, a blend of chaos and art, so bold,
A mesmerizing symphony of hues and shades,
Where passion and creativity cascade.

Your soul, a canvas painted with swirling
emotion,
A masterpiece born from life's wild commotion,
In every brushstroke, there's a story untold,
A kaleidoscope of colors, vibrant and bold.

The chaos within you, a tempest that roars,
A torrential storm that rattles closed doors,
But amidst the chaos, a spark of creation,
A beacon of light, a divine revelation.

Your artistry dances, free and unconfined,
Immersed in the chaos, a serenade of the mind,
You mold your world with artistic finesse,
Creating beauty from life's intricate mess.

I'm captivated by the way your spirit unfurls,
With every twist and turn, my heart twirls,
For within your chaos, there's a celestial grace,
A unique blend of wildness and delicate
embrace.

In your soul's fusion of chaos and art,
I find solace, a connection that sets us apart,
For love thrives within the untamed flame,

Where chaos and art intertwine, unashamed.

So let us revel in the beauty we possess,
In the symphony of chaos and art, let us confess,
That it is in the rawness, the unfiltered essence,
We discover a love that defies all pretense.

For I am enamored with your soul's intricate
design,
A tapestry of chaos and art, so divine,
And in this love, we find our own unique path,
Where chaos and art intertwine, forever to last.

One life not enough

In the fleeting moments of life's embrace,

We wander through time, in a transient space,
With dreams to chase and stories to unfold,
We realize that one life is never long enough to
behold.

Like whispers carried on the wings of the wind,
Our days slip away, leaving memories thinned,
We strive to capture each precious breath,
But time dances swiftly, like a waltz towards
death.

There are mountains to climb and oceans to
explore,
Endless possibilities knocking at our door,
But the hands of the clock never cease their
flight,
Leaving us yearning for more, as day turns to
night.

We gather moments like precious jewels,
But as the tapestry of life gradually unfurls,
We find that one life, no matter how we strive,
Is but a fleeting chapter in the grand narrative of
life.

There are passions to pursue and love to share,
Lessons to learn, burdens to bear,
Yet, as the sun sets on each passing day,

We realize that one life is simply not enough to convey.

We yearn for more time, to savor and explore,
To unlock the mysteries that lie at our core,
To leave our mark upon this vast expanse,
But alas, one life is but a fleeting dance.

So let us embrace each moment with fervent zest,
Knowing that life's brevity puts us to the test,
For in the awareness of our limited stay,
We find the courage to live fully, come what may.

Though one life may not be long enough,
Let us cherish the moments, smooth and rough,
And strive to leave a legacy, deep and true,
In the hearts and souls of those we once knew.

For in the tapestry of existence, we find our place,
Weaving our stories with dignity and grace,
And though one life may never be enough,
We embrace its fleeting beauty, amidst the rough.

You're so easy to love

Your words, like gentle whispers, touch my
soul,
They weave a tapestry of emotions, making me
whole,
In the depths of my being, your love takes flight,
A beacon of warmth, a guiding light.

You see through the layers, the masks that I
wear,
Embracing my flaws, showing me you care,
With every word and gesture, you effortlessly
impart,
A love so pure, it resonates within my heart.

Your love is a melody, soothing and sweet,
A symphony of tenderness, with each heartbeat,
It lifts me up when I'm feeling low,
Filling my world with a vibrant glow.

In your presence, I find solace and ease,
A sanctuary where my worries find release,
Your love wraps around me like a gentle
embrace,
Creating a haven, a sacred space.

You inspire me to grow, to become the best I can
be,
Your unwavering support sets my spirit free,
With you, I feel seen, understood, and known,
A love like yours, I've never before known.

You make loving you so effortless and true,
I'm blessed to have found a love like you,
In your presence, I find peace and tranquility,
For you, my love, make it easy to love
unconditionally.

So let our love dance in the winds of time,
A love that's boundless, a love so sublime,
With each passing day, our connection grows,
A love that's infinite, forever it flows.

Thank you for loving me, so pure and free,
You're the embodiment of love's true beauty,
In your arms, I find my eternal bliss,
For you, my love, are so easy to love, and I'm
grateful for this.

Love and pain... (Part two)

(Verse 1)

In the shadows of my heart, a story unfolds,
A tale of love and pain, the way it always goes,
You came into my life, like a hurricane,
But now I'm left here, drowning in the pouring rain.

(Pre-Chorus)
Every touch, every kiss, felt like heaven at first,
But now I'm lost in a maze, my heart about to burst,
Love's a double-edged sword, cutting deep within,
I'm torn between the pleasure and the pain I'm in.

(Chorus)
Love and pain, a bittersweet symphony,
Two sides of a coin, intertwined in harmony,
I'm dancing in the fire, can't break these chains,
In this love song of ours, love and pain remains.

(Verse 2)
We built castles in the sand, dreams in the sky,
But reality came crashing down, without a reason why,
The promises we made, now shattered on the ground,
I'm left picking up the pieces, lost and never found.

(Bridge)
I'm haunted by the memories, the echoes of your
voice,
The scars upon my heart, aching with no choice,
But through the tears and heartache, I'll find my
way,
For love and pain, they teach us how to truly
stay.

(Chorus)
Love and pain, a bittersweet symphony,
Two sides of a coin, intertwined in harmony,
I'm dancing in the fire, can't break these chains,
In this love song of ours, love and pain remains.

(Chorus)
Love and pain, a bittersweet symphony,
Two sides of a coin, intertwined in harmony,
I'll rise above the ashes, find strength once again,
In this love song of ours, love and pain will end.

(Outro)
Love and pain, they go hand in hand,
But I won't let them define who I am,
I'll heal and learn to love once more,
For in the depths of pain, I'll find love's encore.

Wasted time

*H*ours, where moments fade,
I find myself entangled in a wasteful charade.
Time, a precious currency, slips through my
grasp,
As I wander aimlessly, trapped in a fruitless
clasp.

Oh, the minutes lost, like grains of sand so fine,
Each passing day, a mournful chime.
I watch as the sun dances across the sky,
While my aspirations lazily pass by.

In idle pursuits and distractions galore,
I surrender my essence, craving for more.
The hours dissolve into empty space,
Leaving behind regret, an unwelcome trace.

The allure of procrastination, a siren's call,
Enticing me deeper into this endless sprawl.
Dreams lie dormant, abandoned and cold,
As I dally in the stories I've been told.

Oh, the hours squandered, never to regain,
A symphony of potential drowned in disdain.
I yearn for purpose, for a path to tread,
To reclaim the moments I so recklessly shed.

Yet, in this reflection, a glimmer of light,
A choice to emerge from this self-imposed night.
To awaken the passions that slumber within,

And cease this dance with idle whim.

For time, though elusive, can still be seized,
If only I dare to break free from what appeased.
To chase the dreams that stir my soul's fire,
And embrace the journey, never to tire.

So, let this be a testament to the days gone past,
A reminder of the hours that did not last.
I'll rise from the ashes of wasted time,
And forge a future, purposeful and sublime.

Dream of becoming a poet

In the realm of ink and parchment, where
words take flight,
I dream of weaving verses, of bathing in their
light.
A poet's heart beats within, a fire burning bright,
Guiding me through the darkness, like stars in
the night.

With pen in hand, I dance upon the page,
Crafting sonnets and ballads, releasing my inner
sage.
In the tapestry of language, I find solace and
release,
A sanctuary of emotions, where my soul finds
peace.

I dream of capturing life's essence with each line,
Painting vivid portraits with words so sublime.
From the depths of my being, tales begin to
unfurl,
Whispering secrets, transforming thoughts into a
pearl.

Through metaphors and imagery, I strive to
convey,
The beauty and the chaos, in life's intricate
ballet.
To touch a reader's heart, to ignite their own
dreams,

To unite souls in verse, with each syllable it
seems.

I yearn to wander through realms of imagination,
To explore the realms of love, pain, and elation.
To string together stanzas, like beads on a
string,
Creating a melodic symphony that makes hearts
sing.

But dreams alone won't shape a poet's fate,
It takes courage and dedication, to navigate
Through doubts and uncertainties, to embrace
the unknown,
To let the muse guide me, as my words are sown.

So, I'll continue to dream, to nurture this desire,
To let my voice soar, higher and higher.
For within the realm of poetry, I find my truest
self,
A poet's spirit, forever longing to delve.

And one day, my dreams will blossom and
bloom,
As the world embraces my verses, dispelling all
gloom.
I'll stand proud as a poet, my voice ringing true,
Sharing my soul's whispers, with hearts old and
new.

READERS ARE THE WRITERS MIRROR,
I PERSONALLY WANT TO THANK EVERYONE OF
YOU.. CHECK OUT MY FIRST BOOK A JOURNEY
THOUGH LOVE AND PAIN, IT'S WERE IT'S ALL
STARTED… CAN'T GET ENOUGH THE 3RD ONE
IS COMING SOON.

www.ingramcontent.com/pod-product-compliance
Lightning Source LLC
Chambersburg PA
CBHW052112030426
42335CB00025B/2947